THERE'S A PRAWN IN PARLIAMENT HOUSE

THE KIDS' GUIDE TO AUSTRALIA'S AMAZING DEMOCRACY

ANNABEL CRABB

Illustrated by
First Dog on the Moon

ALLEN&UNWIN
SYDNEY • MELBOURNE • AUCKLAND • LONDON

First published by Allen & Unwin in 2025

Allen & Unwin
Cammeraygal Country
83 Alexander Street
Crows Nest NSW 2065
Australia
Phone: (61 2) 8425 0100
Email: info@allenandunwin.com
Web: www.allenandunwin.com

Allen & Unwin acknowledges the Traditional Owners of the Country on which we live and work. We pay our respects to all Aboriginal and Torres Strait Islander Elders, past and present.

EU Authorised Representative: Easy Access System Europe,
Mustamäe tee 50, 10621 Tallinn, Estonia, gpsr.requests@easproject.com

A catalogue record for this book is available from the National Library of Australia

ISBN 978 1 76063 775 0

For teaching resources, explore allenandunwin.com/learn

Illustration technique: Photoshop on a Wacom tablet

Cover and text design by Kristy Lund-White
Cover illustration by First Dog on the Moon
Annabel Crabb photos by Stephen Blake
Set in 11.5 pt Questa Slab Light by Kristy Lund-White
Printed and bound in Australia by the Opus Group

10 9 8 7

The paper in this book is FSC® certified. FSC® promotes environmentally responsible, socially beneficial and economically viable management of the world's forests.

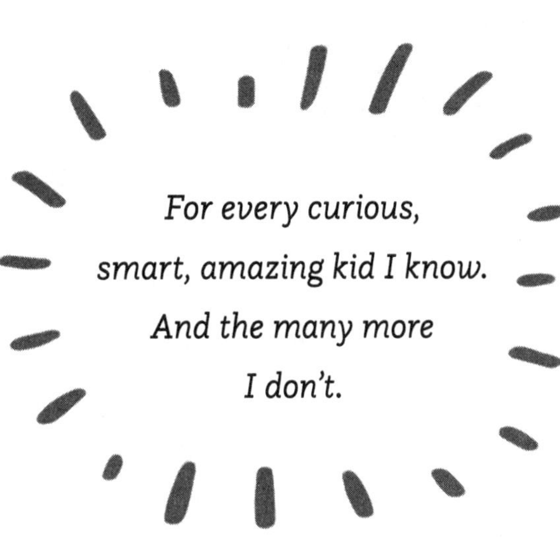

For every curious,
smart, amazing kid I know.
And the many more
I don't.

CONTENTS

AN INTRODUCTORY NOTE FROM SHAWN

I'm too modest to describe myself as a celebrity, exactly, but I do have my own fridge magnet in the parliamentary gift shop, and you would not **BELIEVE** *the number of people who come to admire (okay, step on) me in my role as Largest In-Floor Fossil of the Australian Parliament.*

The continent we call Australia has a long, loooong history. The Australian Federation – our democratic system of government – has only been around since 1901! Before that, Australia was a bunch of colonies and prisons and, before that, for many thousands of years, it was made up of many, many small nations of Indigenous people, with many different languages and ways of governing themselves and sharing the land.

Personally, I have quite a long life story too.

I'm not showing off or anything, but I'm pretty sure I'm the oldest resident of the building! I'm about 350 million years old, champions. Although I look like a shrimp, scientists think I was possibly a piece of coral. But people started calling me 'Shawn the Prawn', and you know what Australia's like: once you get a nickname, it sticks!

I grew up as a young marine invertebrate in the Carboniferous Period, towards the end of the Palaeozoic Era, in an area that we now know as Belgium. My life was fairly unremarkable, I guess. But things really turned around a couple of hundred million years later, when the bit of Belgian black limestone I'm encased in was shipped over to Australia to become part of the geometric patterns on the floor of the Marble Foyer. People really started to notice me!

I love living in Parliament House. Sharing a house with a democracy is awesome! And there are thousands of fascinating humans who work here, from politicians to Hansard reporters to gardeners to librarians to chefs to carpenters to security guards. Plus one horologist, which is the fancy word for someone who fixes clocks. I found that out when I moved here. (This building has more than 2700 clocks, oof.)

Laws are made here. Serious discussions about the best way for our country to work are had here. And by voting in elections, every grown-up Australian is a part of these discussions.

A lot of fascinating people come and go here. I've been stepped on by multiple prime ministers. A governor-general! The President of the United States of America breezed by me once.

But the coolest thing is when school students come to visit me – they are the only people who appreciate me fully, I often think. So it's a huge pleasure to be asked to provide an introduction to this book about how this place works and how our incredible, unique Australian democracy took shape.

I'm leaving you in the hands of a trusted fellow crustacean. Annabel Crabb is a political reporter and TV presenter who has been hanging around the halls of the Parliament for about 25 years! She works for the ABC, and she's going to take you for a tour of the place (I'd take you myself, but I'm encased in some fairly solid sedimentary rock.)

And so it doesn't get too boring, I've also asked my preferred Fossilised Marine Life Cartoonist, First Dog on the Moon, to chime in with some illustrations at crucial points.

Together, they can't promise to tell you absolutely everything about how this country is run, but they'll give it a red-hot go!

And if you happen to visit Parliament House on a school trip or a holiday to Canberra, or if you're dragged here by a politics-obsessed family member (I see a lot of these), please come and say hi!

Your democracy-loving friend,

Shawn

Any words in bold
with an asterisk have been
added as a definition in
the glossary at the back of
the book. Check it out!

1 WELCOME TO PARLIAMENT HOUSE

Australia's government is a democracy. And the whole idea of democracy is that big groups of people – in order to make things easier – elect a small group of representatives to get together and make decisions on behalf of everyone else. We call that group of representatives our Parliament.

Our Parliament is made up of two 'Houses'. They're called the **House of Representatives*** (or the Lower House), and the **Senate*** (or the Upper House). This makes the Australian Parliament a **bicameral parliament.*** Actually, the 'Houses' are just big grand rooms, both found inside the enormous flag-topped building that we call 'Parliament House'.

A parliament with only one chamber is called a **unicameral parliament,*** *which makes it sound more like a mythical horse than it really is.*

Lots of parliamentary systems around the world are bicameral, like Australia. But there are plenty of unicameral ones too. Like China, which has one house in its Parliament, with nearly 3000 members. But China only has one political party. It's not a democracy, which keeps debates *very* simple. Most of the Australian state parliaments are also bicameral, but Queensland – a state that delights in being different – abolished its Upper House after the Labor Government got annoyed with it. In March 1922, the members of the Queensland Legislative Council officially voted to abolish themselves. The room where they used to sit is still there. They use it for special parties and meetings.

Before we plunge into the nitty-gritty of voting, how laws are made, Australia's Constitution and all that stuff, I thought I would give you a tour of the unique building in which all this takes place.

THE HOUSE

Parliament House is built into a hollowed-out hill overlooking Canberra, Australia's capital city. One million cubic metres of earth were excavated to make way for it when it was built in the 1980s. It's ***HUGE*** – it has more than 4500 rooms – but it also has grass running up over the roof, so bits of it look like the hill's still there. You can't miss its crowning feature: the 81-metre flagpole that is one of the largest steel structures in the world and weighs 220 tonnes, which you would know if you could be bothered taking it off and weighing it. Locals sometimes call it the Coathanger because that's what it looks like: a large, dignified coathanger with an Australian flag the size of a double-decker bus on top.

'Canberra' in derived from the Ngunnawal word 'Kambri', meaning 'meeting place'. Local Indigenous people have gathered on these lands for tens of thousands of years.

The flag weighs 22 kilograms and is changed once a month. Two specially qualified workers strap themselves into a tiny, terrifying, custom-built elevator the size of a *very* small wardrobe that hauls them up the steel mast to the wind-whipped top where they have the extremely scary task of putting up a nice fresh flag. Another person below controls the elevator. There are about 14 flags in circulation. They get very tattered very quickly, so after each flag is taken down it is patched and repaired carefully before its next flight!

But it's what happens *under* the flag that's important. Parliament House is where our national system of decision-making happens. The **Prime Minister*** works there, as do the 225 other Members of Parliament we elect on Election Day. Plus about 5000 other people including cleaners, chamber attendants, advisers, researchers, journalists, security guards, spies, camera operators, childcare workers, librarians, lawyers, gardeners, press secretaries, hairdressers, electricians, carpenters, cooks, waiters, **Hansard*** reporters, restorers, turf specialists, laundry workers, postal workers, art experts, bakers, historians, beekeepers, maintenance workers, logistics experts and more.

We often call the Prime Minister 'PM' for short. Likewise 'MP' for Member of Parliament and House of Representatives often gets shortened to 'Reps'.

We don't know exactly who they are, but they're there. FOR SURE.

The main decisions of the Parliament are made in the ***House of Representatives*** and the ***Senate*** – the two big fancy meeting rooms I mentioned earlier, where politicians gather to have debates. I'll explain the difference between the two chambers a bit later in the book when we describe how laws are made, but for now all you need to remember is that the House of Representatives is decorated in green leather and carpet and has 150 members while the Senate is decorated in red leather and carpet and has 76 members.

The carpet detail – ***green*** for the House of Representatives, ***red*** for the Senate – is worth remembering because it makes it easier to navigate around Parliament House, which is famously one of the easiest places in Australia in which to get lost. If you do ever get lost there, just look down. If the carpet under your feet is red, you're in the Senate wing. If it's green, you're on the Reps side. (If it's blue, look out! You're in the Executive Wing, the bit of the building where the Prime Minister and all the **ministers*** work. It's ***VERY*** closely watched, so in all likelihood if you are standing on blue carpet, you are about to meet a security officer!)

As well as having more than 4500 rooms, Parliament House has 22 kilometres of corridors. Many of these corridors look a lot like each other, which is why the carpet tip is important. Hung around the corridors and in the offices is the Parliamentary art collection, which has lots of distinctive modern works.

> ***The art gets moved around a bit, which is why it's not helpful to use an interesting sculpture in Parliament House for navigational purposes. Next week, it might be somewhere else.***

If you were a bird flying over Parliament House, you'd notice that the building is constructed in the shape of a cross. If you're a human looking at the building from the public entrance at the front, under your feet is the Forecourt – a big open space, with a beautiful mosaic based on an artwork by Kumantje (Michael Nelson) Jagamara AM called *Possum and Wallaby Dreaming*. The House of Representatives and all its Members of Parliament's offices are on the left-hand side of the building. On the right is the Senate wing, which also houses the **Press Gallery**,* a corridor on the second floor containing all the journalists, producers and camera operators who work for the media.

Their offices are the easiest to spot because they are the noisiest and – as a journalist I'm very sorry to say this – also the messiest.

And ahead of you but way up the back is the Executive Wing, where the Prime Minister hangs out, along with all the ministers. They get larger, nicer offices than the ordinary Members of Parliament, because ministers have more staff. (They also get first pick of the art collection.) At the exact centre of the building is a fountain under a glass atrium. If you look up you can see the flag right above you.

Key

1. Prime Minister
2. Cabinet Room
3. House of Representatives
4. Members' Hall
5. Senate
6. Press Gallery (second floor)
7. Great Hall
8. Marble Foyer
9. Childcare centre
10. Main Entrance
11. Aussies Café
12. Forecourt

Back door (ministers only)

House of Representatives entrance

Senate entrance

1 2 3 4 5 6 7 8 9 10 11 12

Front door (public entrance)

One cool thing about the building's design is that in theory you can open all the doors from the grand public entrance all the way to the PM's entrance and see through the entire building.

Here's how it works. The front double doors opens onto the spectacular Marble Foyer, and then the next double doors open onto the Great Hall (where all the big dinners and events happen in Parliament), and then another set of doors open on to the Members' Hall, at the centre of which is the water feature. The next doors open into a bunch of committee rooms, and then the next doors after those open into the top-secret Cabinet Room where the ministers meet and make decisions, and then the next doors after those open into the Prime Minister's Office, and then the next doors after *those* go into the Prime Minister's Courtyard.

As you can imagine, these doors are never opened all at once because every single security officer in the building (and there are heaps) would have an instant heart attack. But the designers of Parliament House made it that way because they loved the idea of transparency – that, even though the business of Parliament is complicated, it should be possible to see right through the building all the way to the office of the Prime Minister. This is the same reason the building is set into a hill, with grass all over the top. The designers felt it was important that ordinary voters should be able to walk all over Parliament House. It's a fun reminder that in any democracy, power begins and ends with ordinary people.

SECURITY

When Parliament House was first constructed, little glassed-in security huts were installed around the perimeter roads so that guards could sit in them and keep watch. They were then abandoned almost immediately. It turns out that a person sitting in a brightly lit glass hut at night is kind of... vulnerable. But they are part of the original design, and the original design of Parliament House is honoured to a fault, so they have never been removed. If you are visiting Parliament House, keep an eye out for them. They still have 1980s phones inside!

Parliament House has always been protected by security guards, but the level of protection has been increased very noticeably over the years for a number of reasons including these interesting moments.

In 1992, a man called Clifton Courtney Moss drove his Mitsubishi Pajero about 1000 kilometres from a town called Broken Hill and ploughed it through the great front doors and all the way into the Great Hall. Bollards were installed after that.

Security was tightened further after 1996, when thousands of union demonstrators protesting against the new Liberal Government of John Howard broke into the building and went on a rampage, breaking lots of stuff.

The threat of international terrorism drove a series of major security upgrades from 2001 onwards, including the installation of a steel fence blocking the rooftop from unauthorised visitors.

You can still get to the roof if you enter through security. You just can't run up there and roll down the grass anymore. This is a sad development, because people used to love doing that. But security comes first.

UNDER THE HOUSE

Arguably the coolest thing about Parliament House is that a big chunk of it is underground. Below the House of Representatives and Senate chambers and the public areas lies a secret network of subterranean corridors, accessible only to parliamentary workers.

When I say 'secret', it's because the corridors feel secret, though they're technically not a secret, it's just that not everyone can go and see them. On second thought: I'm sticking with secret. Sounds cooler.

A lot of work happens down there. There are offices and storerooms, huge industrial laundries and kitchens, a full carpentry workshop and a big postal sorting office.

So much mail arrives at Parliament House, and it all has to be sorted and directed, including mail for dead prime ministers.

Every petition that's ever been sent into Parliament is kept down there. Even the art collection lives there in an archive. It's so big and vast, workers get around on electric buggies that haul trailers of documents, recycling and supplies for the Parliament. And every single thing that comes into Parliament House – pallets of water bottles, fresh food, flower arrangements, the mail, even the coffee for the coffee shop and the toilet paper for the hundreds of parliamentary toilets! – has to be scanned or X-rayed at the underground security entrance.

And everything that leaves Parliament House has to come out the same way. Food scraps from the dining rooms and cafés are packaged up, hauled out of the security entrance and sent to a local worm farm.

The underground tunnels are also a super-fast way to get from one side of the building to another. If the Prime Minister is in the Cabinet Room, for example, and required at the main entrance to welcome an official guest, they might be brought down to the basement and whisked across by electric buggy rather than walking through the above-ground halls and being stopped for a million selfies. Something to remember, if you ever become Prime Minister and find yourself pressed for time.

THE CATHEDRAL

Now this really is a secret that even lots of people working in the Parliament don't know about. When Parliament House was being built in the 1980s, ***the money ran out***. This often happens with giant construction projects, and when Parliament House was being built, it was the most expensive building in Australian history. So, bits of it like some of the landscaping ended up being...unfinished. And underground, there is one corner of the building that is just a big gaping hole.

Those in the know call this space 'the Cathedral'. You open a door from an underground corridor and suddenly you're standing on dirt and rubble and gazing at the raw walls and wondering where the heck you are. ***It's wild!*** I was allowed to poke around in there once and there was still stuff lying around that the builders had left, including an old work boot, a newspaper from 1987, even an old cigarette packet with no health warnings on it, which is definitely a very serious antique.

I think it's kind of awesome that the building's still unfinished. It's a good reminder that nothing's perfect, especially where democracies are concerned.

GARDENS

Parliament House was designed to be full of light. Nearly every above-ground office looks out onto some sky, or a courtyard, or a garden. This was deliberate: the designers wanted people working in the building never to forget the world outside. It's a huge part of the building's appeal – wherever you are in Parliament House, you're never far from a beautifully maintained oasis of green in which you can sit and chat. But the designers of the place also knew that **Parliament is full of secrets**. So, if you wander through the courtyards around the parliamentary chambers, you'll notice that wherever there's space to sit and chat, there's also a splishy-splashy fountain. Why? They're there so that nosey individuals can't eavesdrop on what the important-looking people on the next bench are saying!

Give it a try, if you visit. Can you eavesdrop? I bet you'll struggle!

Parliament's gardeners are highly trained and *very* passionate about their work. From the 'turfies' who keep the lawns in perfect condition all year round to the horticulturalists who monitor the 4500 trees and 135,000 plants both indoors and out, everyone on the gardening team has an important job to do to maintain the 23 hectares of landscaped gardens.

BIRDS

Everything about Parliament House is very carefully designed. But you know what you can't control, even when you design things very carefully? Yep: nature. Parliament House is patrolled by a very intense crew of magpies and currawongs. They cannot be overcome. They make their own rules. And they rule the courtyards. If you pop out to a courtyard table with your lunch, the magpies will steal a hot chip from your plate whether you are the Prime Minister or a visiting school student. This is a good reminder of the democratic spirit. I was once assured by a long-serving security guard that one of the parliamentary magpies can say ***'hello!'*** So when you visit, make sure you say 'hello!' to every magpie you encounter. I've talked to every bird I've seen, but have never found this special magpie, so let me know if you ever find it and converse with it.

In 2019, the ranks of parliamentary birds were joined by a gang of ducks, drawn to the courtyards of Parliament by the availability of food and the plentiful fountains. Unfortunately, ducks do *very* slimy poos, I regret to say, and they are *not* picky about where. So, as duck numbers swelled,

the groundskeepers declared war on them by bringing in a peregrine falcon called Floyd, just to make them feel a bit less comfortable.

The ducks got the message and retreated to Lake Burley Griffin. An uneasy truce prevails to this day.

Invading Insects

Another way the natural world regularly reminds the Australian Parliament who was there first – moths. When Canberra was selected in the late 1800s as the site for the new nation's capital, none of the people in charge knew that it was smack-bang in the middle of the migration path of a fleshy insect called *Agrotis infusa*, more commonly known as the bogong moth. Most moths aren't migratory, but the bogong moth is. These critters breed on the plains west of the Great Dividing Range in south-eastern Queensland and northern New South Wales, but they don't like the heat. So, in October and November, when things start hotting up, they set out for the cool of the Snowy Mountains south of Canberra, where they hang out in caves and crevices for the summer before flying home in autumn.

When Parliament House was completed in the late 1980s and Queen Elizabeth II came to open the building, the flag was raised and the whole structure was floodlit so that the flag would be proudly visible night and day.

Then, and only then, was it realised that, while to a human being this building might signify the finest in Australian democratic process, to a moth it looks a lot like **Moth Disneyland**.

Moths are drawn to lights, and Parliament House is basically a bright beacon right in the middle of the moths' migration path. So of course millions of them stop by, and in particularly mothy years, they get inside the building in vast numbers and set off fire alarms and blunder into people's meals and drinks and even occasionally people's *mouths* if they're talking a lot.

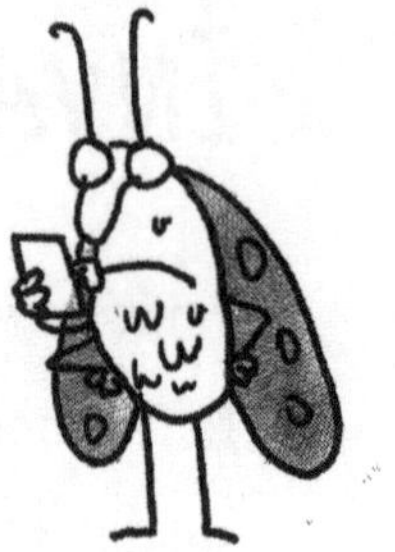

The bogong moth is significant to Aboriginal communities, particularly the local Ngunnawal and Ngambri peoples. Roasted on fires, the moths have been a tasty and nutritious treat for thousands of years. But swallowing a live one when it flies into your mouth unexpectedly can be quite a shock.

The sight of great piles of moths being swept away from doors and windows is not an uncommon one in Canberra, so be ready for it if you visit the Parliament in spring. And maybe ***keep your mouth shut***.

LIBRARY

The Parliamentary Library, like your school library, contains books. Except this is a special library because it doesn't *just* house and collect books. It's full of very smart, studious souls called parliamentary librarians, who are also research specialists. Librarians research and compose papers on all sorts of weird and wonderful topics. One of the best things about being a Member of Parliament or **Senator*** is that you're allowed to ring up the Library and ask a librarian to research pretty much ***anything you want***. This is necessary because an MP deals with a blistering array of issues, from 'is it a good idea to put a wind farm here' to 'trade disputes with the federated states of Micronesia'. The parliamentary librarians stand ready to help time-poor MPs get up to speed, quickly, on things they might know nothing about.

Sadly, journalists are *not* allowed to ring up and ask for research assistance, which causes me to weep salty tears. But anyone is allowed to go to the Australian Parliament House website and trawl through their hundreds of thousands of endlessly helpful and fascinating research briefs.

HANSARD

If you sit in the public galleries and gaze down upon the chambers, you will notice a couple people who aren't MPs seated at the central bench, gazing intently at laptops. They are the Hansard reporters. Hansard is the record of everything that is said in Parliament. In the old days, they used to take handwritten shorthand notes of the proceedings, later to be transcribed and bound in great volumes. Now, the Hansard is prepared super-quickly and is available online, usually by the following day! If you go to the Australian Parliament House website and look at 'Hansard', you'll find all the debates. ***This record is hugely important.*** MPs can always be held accountable for what they've said in the Parliament, and old debates can tell us a lot about how issues have been discussed and decided in our past. These days, Hansard reporters are assisted by all sorts of modern technology that allows for very speedy transcription, but they still monitor and check what they hear, according to strict Hansard conventions and rules.

One thing you'll notice if you sit in on the Parliament – particularly in **Question Time*** – is that there is a considerable amount of shouting and heckling. The parliamentary term for this is 'interjecting' – though of course it amounts to what my grandmother would have called 'yahooing', and, let's be honest, if you tried carrying on like that you'd probably get sent to the principal's office fairly smartly.

The Hansard rules on interjections are as follows: the official transcript of the day's debate will *not* include interjections unless the person officially speaking responds to the interjection. Or if the **Speaker*** (who chairs the House of Representatives) or the **President*** (who chairs the Senate) responds. So, responding to a taunt can be a delicate strategic question. ***Do you want what they said to go on the record?***

*Let's say the Member for Whistlenose is on her feet banging on about something and the Member for Stinkfinger is trying to knock her off her game by yelling, 'Thou art a most notable coward, an infinite and endless liar, an hourly promise breaker, the owner of no one good quality!'**

**Note: This insult is borrowed from Shakespeare, so it's of a slightly higher quality than you usually hear in the Parliament.*

If the Member for Whistlenose just ploughs on and ignores these attacks, they won't be recorded in the Hansard. But if she replies, say: 'I know you are, but what am I?' then the entire exchange will be recorded.

Sometimes if the MP speaking hears an *unwise* taunt – one that definitely goes **too far** – they may ask the Speaker to force the taunter to withdraw the comment. This has the delicious effect of the Speaker's reprimand going on the official record.

If you ever watch an energetic Question Time, you'll note that Parliament has a massive dobbing culture. It's really something.

A draft of the Hansard record is circulated each day to MPs, so that they can check that their words have been recorded accurately. The Hansard reporters correct minor grammatical errors and iron out stammering or repetition, if to do so creates a clearer account of what was said. But if you're an MP who reads the draft Hansard and realises too late that you've said something absolutely ridiculous, it is *bad form* to attempt to edit out what you actually said.

As one of the early state MPs in the Victorian Parliament is said once to have advised a newcomer: 'Hansard was meant to preserve the idiom of Parliament…not the idiots.'

CHILDCARE CENTRE

Parliament House is like a mini-city. There are cafés, a bookshop, a gym, a swimming pool, squash courts, even a hairdresser! But for a long time, there wasn't a childcare centre. This is because when the building was being designed most MPs were men, and if they were dads they usually had wives who looked after their children. In 1983, Ros Kelly was the first woman to have a baby while serving as a member of the House of Representatives. And she found it a big juggle. Nobody else tried it for quite a while after that!

But as more women came into the Parliament, questions started being asked more pointedly, such as: 'Why does this building have squash courts but no childcare centre?' And 'Wouldn't childcare on site make things easier for parents working Parliament's famously long hours?'

There were arguments, debates, feasibility studies. It took years. Finally, the decision was taken to rebuild the ground-level parliamentary bar, rip out the beer taps, put in some teeny-tiny toilets and voila! A childcare centre. Kids now have a place to be looked after while their parents are working in Parliament House. ***Hooray!***

SHAWN THE PRAWN

You've already met my favourite part of Parliament House. It's in the ***Marble Foyer*** – the very grand entrance foyer inside the main entrance, which has a vast black and white stone floor and 48 pale pink and green marble columns designed to remind you of being in a gum tree forest. It's beautiful. If you ever visit Parliament House, don't forget to look up and see the incredible wood panels featuring images of native Australian flowers made of intricate filigreed native timbers. But to see the tiny, accidental highlight of this room, you have to look down.

The shiny black parts of the Marble Foyer's floor are made from limestone imported from Belgium. Inside the stone are all sorts of bits and pieces including tiny ***fossils***. And if you look at the first step of the mighty staircase sweeping you up to the first floor where the Queen's Terrace Café is, you'll find a a little coral fossil, about the size of a 20-cent coin, that looks like a perfectly preserved shrimp. Somebody – history doesn't record who – christened him ***Shawn***. Shawn the Prawn.

Shawn is estimated to be 350 million years old, and now he's a superstar of Australian democracy!

2

HOW DID WE GET HERE?

The first thing to remember is that the Australia we live in, with its cities and roads and health system and universities and sometimes-dodgy internet, is – in historical terms – ***extremely new***.

Humans have been living on this continent for up to 60,000 years. The current Australian democratic system was only installed in 1901. So, this whole show has been our way of doing things for just one four-hundred-and-fiftieth of the time that this landmass has had people walking around on it. To put it another way, if you drew a one-metre-long timeline to tell the story of human life in what we now call Australia, our glorious Federation with its bicameral parliament only shows up in the last two centimetres!

One Continent, Two Systems

It's not easy to summarise the system of self-governance that First Nations people had before their home of 60,000 years was taken over by British colonists beginning with the First Fleet.

That's because Aboriginal people did not have a written national constitution or parliament. This does not mean Aboriginal people did not have systems of government and laws at that time. They did. It's just that these systems did not resemble the systems that the colonists recognised. If you visit the website of the Australian Institute of Aboriginal and Torres Strait Islander Studies, you can see a map of Aboriginal Australia showing all the different nations. You'll probably know the names of a few of them – certainly the name of the place where your school is, for starters. Each of these Aboriginal nations have their own languages and traditions, so you can't really summarise and compare First Nations government with today's federal Parliament in Canberra – it's apples and oranges.

But there are some broad differences definitely worth pointing out.

The biggest one is that while First Nations culture includes a complex system of laws, with consequences for breaking them, the laws are not debated and legislated in the same way they are in the federal Parliament.

In our **Westminster-style democracy,*** we have elections every three years to elect politicians who make new laws.

In First Nations government, the laws don't change; they are ancient, and meshed deeply in the care of and relationship to Country. Leaders have the responsibility to maintain and hand down the law, and educate younger generations. Laws aren't written down in legislation, but learned and coded and passed down in conversation and song and ritual.

Among the most important documents in Australian history are the Yirrkala bark petitions, written and painted by the Yolŋu People of Arnhem Land in the Northern Territory and sent to the Menzies Government in 1963. The Menzies Government had agreed to let a French mining company dig for bauxite on the Yolŋu People's land. Yolŋu leaders came together and – in an attempt to make sense of this distant government and its decisions – wrote a petition to the Parliament asking politely for the mining not to occur. This was a very significant moment, where the Aboriginal system of government clashed with the federal Parliament in Canberra, which had decided in 1902 that Aboriginal people shouldn't be allowed to vote. This right was not restored until 1962, but it wasn't until 1984 that First Nations people were required to enrol and vote in elections.

The Yirrkala bark petitions were the beginning of the Aboriginal land rights movement in Australia – a struggle that continues ***to this very day***. Aboriginal people never agreed to give away rights to the land that had always been theirs.

In late 2024, the **High Court*** of Australia finally ruled that the Yolŋu People should be compensated for the mining activity that took place on their land without their consent, all those years ago.

A Potted History of Australia

50,000 years BCE to 1788

Australia is occupied by a vast network of Aboriginal clans. They are related to each other and governed by culture and song, and intricate laws dictating movement, marriage and rites of passage. Navigation is done by astronomy and song. Agriculture and aquaculture are well developed, and hundreds of different languages are spoken across the continent.

1788–1901

Europeans arrive and decide the place would be good to take over. English colonial governors arrive with fleets of **convicts,*** and free settlers looking for land. They bring a penal (criminal justice) system, guns, domesticated animals, alcohol, disease and European crops. Aboriginal landowners are in many cases displaced by violence. Colonies are established and run by the British Colonial Office on the other side of the world. From the 1840s onwards, some colonies start to run their own elections with the permission of the British Empire.

1901–present

Westminster-style democracy.

This book is mainly about these last two centimetres of our timeline. To understand how it works and why it's so unique, we have to look back at the complicated and fascinating story of how it came to be designed.

FROM FIRST FLEET TO FEDERATION

Back in the mid-1700s England (also known, along with its neighbour Scotland, as Great Britain) was (and there is no polite way to say this) an absolute ***bin fire***.

Actually, that's not quite fair. Some things were going well. People were living longer than in the previous century. Health care was coming along. Fewer women died in childbirth. Agriculture was flourishing across Britain and people had food to eat. The Industrial Revolution had begun, generating a new era of prosperity and production of goods. Now, I know what you're thinking: where's the bin fire? Hooray for food and stuff, and not dying of the plague!

And yes, those were all good things. But the awkward downside of people not dying young swiftly became obvious, especially in London: ***hideous overcrowding***. Britain's population *doubled* between 1750 and 1850.

But Britain's social problems were about more than just overcrowding. As the Industrial Revolution cranked up and humans got better at making stuff like clothes and hats and kitchenware and tools, there was also suddenly more things to steal. Whole new categories of crime emerged, like smuggling, horse rustling and highway robbery. The result was that prisons overflowed.

The Gin Acts of 1700s*

In the first half of the 1700s, British people had also discovered a very powerful alcoholic spirit called gin. By the 1730s, average gin consumption among Londoners was one litre a week! It was generally agreed that the gin craze did not help people make good decisions. Britain passed several 'Gin Acts' to reduce consumption, but crime rates nonetheless went through the roof. All these people getting drunk on gin and making bad decisions like stealing had to be locked up. This is an important lesson in government. Sometimes, in a large population, one problem (in this case, too much gin) helps generate another problem (in this case, overflowing prisons).

The British Government cycled through some imaginative ideas for what to do with this excess of convicts. There was the death penalty, which was obviously an extremely effective means of reducing the prisoner population. The death penalty applied to a wide range of crimes.

Obviously murder and **treason*** *were on the list, but so were smaller crimes like stealing, cutting down a tree, and robbing a rabbit warren (not even joking).*

The government also experimented with locking up prisoners on 'hulks' – disused ships that were moored on the River Thames. But the solution that offered all the permanence of execution with none of the mess was 'deportation', which meant popping the criminals on ocean-going boats and shipping them off to British colonies around the world.

The British Empire at this time was extremely powerful, and had a well-deserved reputation for conquering distant countries and raiding them for land and treasures (stealing everything from priceless artworks to exotic birds to provide plumage for the fancy hats of well-to-do English ladies), and even sometimes stealing human beings to work as slaves. These colonies on distant lands were also viewed as handy ***dumping grounds*** for unwanted British humans. Nice, hey.

America was a favoured destination for British convicts for a while. But when the American Revolution kicked off in 1775, the rebels in America had no interest in accepting any further British criminals. Aha! Time to find a new place to put the baddies. How fortuitous, then, that the British Empire became aware of a promising landmass Down Under. The British explorer James Cook wasn't the first European to stumble across this vast continent, but he had officially claimed it for Great Britain on 22 August 1770. Encouraged, the British Government dispatched 11 ships that came to be known as the 'First Fleet'. Between them, the ships carried nearly 1400 colonists and convicts, as well as countless rats, cockroaches and fleas, and domestic animals like dogs, cats, pigs, cows and rabbits. They made landfall in January 1788.

The youngest convict aboard the First Fleet was 13-year-old John Hudson. He was nine when he was convicted of burglary.

Arguably the pettiest offender was a man called Benjamin Ingram. He was a pickpocket, and he had been convicted and deported for stealing a single linen handkerchief. ***Harsh!***

Exporting criminals to this new southern land solved a big problem for lawmakers in Britain, but it created a lot of new problems in what would come to be known as Australia.

The biggest and most long-lasting problem is something that has never been fixed. The arrival of the First Fleet brought terrible dislocation, violence, disruption and death to many of the humans who were already living in Australia, who had been minding their own business for tens of thousands of years.

The colonists didn't count the Indigenous population of Australia as humans or recognise their claim to the land. They commonly shot and killed Aboriginal people who resisted them. And even where peaceful co-existence occurred, it was not on equal terms.

To this day, Australia's First Peoples have shorter life expectancy, poorer health and worse access to education and housing, despite being the oldest continuous culture in the world.

The First Fleet carried more than just British colonists with guns to the continent. It also brought diseases unknown to the First Nations inhabitants, and strange new animals, like cats and rats and rabbits, all of which in turn created devastating new and far-reaching problems.

The rabbits aboard the First Fleet were brought along for their meat and fur. At first they were kept securely in cages. But in 1859, a farmer called Thomas Austin released 13 rabbits on his property in Barwon Park, Victoria. He loved shooting, and he set the animals free in the hope that they would breed so he and his friends could have fun gunning them down. ***It worked.*** Seven years later, hunters killed 14,000 rabbits at Barwon Park.

But then it worked too well. Over the ensuing century, rabbits spread relentlessly across the country. They ate crops and decimated ground cover, causing terrible soil erosion that contributed to the decline in native plant and animal species.

By the 1940s, there were an estimated *600 million* rabbits in Australia. All because Thomas Austin had fancied a bit of target practice. This is another lesson for governments, and humans. Sometimes tiny decisions have huge consequences.

The **penal colony*** of New South Wales (NSW) was the first to be established after the First Fleet's arrival. It was ruled by a British chap called Arthur Phillip, who commanded the First Fleet and became the colony's first Governor. Over the years, in other bits of what the British gradually realised was a pretty huge landmass, more colonies were established. These were in the parts of Australia we now know as Tasmania, Queensland, Western Australia, South Australia and Victoria. In each the British established settlements, which grew into towns, which grew into cities, and were ruled by governors sent over from Britain. Some of these colonies comprised free British settlers and others featured convicts, but they were all under the control of the British Government, whose headquarters were up to a four-month sail away.

In those days, nobody voted in Australia, and the rules and decisions were all made in London. The British Government had something called 'The Colonial Office', which ran the British colonies all around the world. British soldiers guarded the colonies and kept order. Governors sent from Britain ruled each colony and regularly reported by letters and bulletins back to London.

Everything changed in 1843, when the first Australian colonial election was held. This election was in NSW, to establish a Legislative Council to advise the Governor. It was a wild affair – there was a riot. Shots were fired. A gang of outraged whalers retrieved some blubber shovels from their ship for fighting with. A man was bludgeoned to death. But at the end of the election 24 members were elected to the new Legislative Council.

And the Governor reported back to London that the election '*went off very well*'.

Only men who owned property were eligible to vote in this election. And voting mostly happened at the pub. **Candidates*** bought beer for the voters, which was called **'treating'**.

The secret ballot is an Australian invention. The first ever elections held by secret ballot were in Victoria in 1856. Known at the time as the Australian Ballot, its use spread around the world.

So, to get elected you just went to the pub and bought enough beers for people to get the job. Any questions? This sounds like an Australian innovation, but it was actually heavily based on the British method of voting at that time.

In 1850, though, the *Australian Colonies Government Act* was passed by the British Parliament, which allowed the Australian colonies to form their own governments.

Self-government was formally granted to New South Wales, Victoria and Tasmania in 1855, South Australia in 1856, Queensland in 1859 and Western Australia in 1890.

A Golden Plot Twist

In the mid-1800s, gold was discovered in Australia, which triggered something called the Gold Rush. Many fortune-seekers jumped on ships to voyage Down Under in the hope of unearthing a nugget that would make them instantly rich.

In between 1850 and 1870, just 20 years, the population of Australia *quadrupled*! And if you think there were consequences when the rabbit population exploded...well. It was even more complicated when human numbers multiplied so quickly.

The young colonial governments had their work cut out for them. So many new issues and challenges to manage! And because of the Gold Rush, suddenly so many people! And because the six self-governing colonies each had their own governments, and their own laws, and their own tax systems, and their own way of doing things, you can imagine how confusing things got.

The colonies all had different rules about who could vote, too. In those days, women couldn't vote in any of them. Not all colonies specifically barred Aboriginal voters, but Indigenous people were never sought out to be placed on the electoral roll. And Tasmania, with its high proportion of convicts, only allowed property owners the vote, a rule which was retained until 1900!

Each of the colonies made its own decisions about defence, transport, healthcare systems and so on. Communication between the colonies was not great, and it was further complicated by the necessity of relying on advice from London, which took months to arrive by ship. Also, the colonies taxed each other.

If you ran a hat shop in Melbourne and you wanted to sell your hats in Sydney, you'd have to pay a tariff – or tax – to the New South Wales government when you hauled your hats over the border. Or bricks, or hay, or whatever else you were selling. It was chaos.

If you want an example of ***Peak Absurdity*** achieved by this messy model of colonial government, look no further than trains.

Trains were very important in colonial Australia because the distances between cities were so huge, there weren't cars or trucks or planes, and there's only so much stuff you can ask a horse to carry. Building rail lines between population centres was an urgent priority.

But when the colonies built their railways, they each used different models of train – which meant they each built the tracks different widths apart (known as **rail gauges***). Queensland's tracks were laid 1.06 metres apart, New South Wales's were 1.44 metres apart, and Victoria's were 1.6 metres apart.

This meant that trains could not go all the way from Sydney to Melbourne, for instance. Instead, a train would go from Sydney to Albury (on the border between New South Wales and Victoria), then the goods aboard would be completely unloaded and reloaded onto a Victorian train to travel on a Victorian track the rest of the way to Melbourne. Even more annoyingly, passengers and luggage would be searched at the border just to make sure nobody was trying to sneak hats through without paying the proper tariffs.

This variation in gauge continued to be a headache for another century, through two world wars, and it eventually cost an eye-watering amount of money to correct.

The whole railway debacle was a powerful argument in favour of the six colonies coming together and co-operating as a group, an idea they started kicking around towards the end of the 1800s. By this time, it was a century since the British had helped themselves to the continent. Seventy per cent of the population of Australia had been born here. Generations of British immigrants and their descendants began to feel that they had more in common with each other than they did with distant Britain.

And the colonies had a lot more in common with each other than with other countries. They faced the same challenges. How to trade with other nations? How to defend themselves? How to communicate with each other? How to farm and mine and make a profit off the land they shared?

DESIGNING A NEW NATION

In 1889, the **Premier*** of New South Wales, Sir Henry Parkes, gave a stirring speech urging the colonies to come together as a nation, speaking of the '*crimson thread of kinship that runs through us all*'. Then in 1890, Melbourne hosted the Australasian Federation Conference (New Zealanders were invited too).

The following year, there was a second federation convention in Sydney. It went on for five weeks, was chaired by Edmund Barton (who would go on to become Australia's first Prime Minister) and started getting into the nitty-gritty of what an

Australian constitution would look like and how a parliament would work. The participants took ideas from everywhere.

It was exciting stuff. But then a bunch of unrelated crises hit, which took the air out of the Federation balloon. In 1890, there was a maritime workers' strike. In 1891, a shearers' strike. In 1892, a miners' strike! These were all huge industries back then, so the strikes really knocked the economy around, and in 1893 a series of banks collapsed. So, the colonial governments got distracted. They were too busy putting out all the other fires.

But then something interesting happened. The people took matters into their own hands!

A feeling of nationalism and urgency – partially inspired by campaigning newspapers and a generation of Australian artists who took pride in painting uniquely Australian scenes – gave the movement a new lift, and a series of people's conventions was staged around the country. Political leaders refocused on the task, and at official conventions in 1897 and 1898 the outline of Australia's new federation took shape.

It wasn't easy, because the less populous states were very worried that NSW and Victoria – the more populous and therefore more powerful states – would bully and dominate them. Western Australia in particular was extremely cautious. Gold had just been discovered there, and the small population of the most far-flung Australian colony had low enthusiasm for handing over their new-found prosperity and independence to a gang of bossy boots from the eastern colonies. When the draft of the Australian Constitution was finalised, Western Australians still weren't decided about whether to join.

Awkwardly, because all the colonies were still officially under British rule, they needed laws to be passed in the British Parliament before Federation could happen. And on 5 July 1900, the *Commonwealth of Australia Constitution Act* passed the British Parliament. Queen Victoria rubber-stamped it on 9 July, and three weeks after that, Western Australia held a **referendum*** and agreed that they would sign up too. Federation was *go!*

The new Federation would be proclaimed on 1 January 1901. The British Government and Queen Victoria chose John Hope, the seventh Earl of Hopetoun, to be the new nation's first **Governor-General.*** They gave him the Order of the Thistle and popped him on a ship for Australia.

The Order of the Thistle is a very fancy honour that the monarch bestows on an individual to acknowledge their service. They get to wear a special brooch and hat.

Unfortunately, the journey did not go well. Lord Hopetoun stopped off in India and caught typhoid fever. He didn't arrive in Australia until mid-December. And when he got off the ship, he was still pretty sick and – more problematically – had no idea how to approach his one job as Australia's first Governor-General, which was to appoint an acting Prime Minister.

The plan was to create the Federation and then have the first elections, but to create the Federation Australia needed to have an acting Prime Minister. Lord Hopetoun just chose the Premier of the oldest state – New South Wales – to be the acting Prime Minister. Understandable, especially from someone still a bit woozy with typhoid. But the problem was that the NSW Premier, Sir William Lyne, had actually been a long-term opponent of Federation. Plus, he was disliked by just about everybody. Nobody was willing to serve in his government. As the days ticked by towards the official Federation date of 1 January, Australia experienced its first constitutional crisis! It's now known as 'The Hopetoun Blunder'.

Finally, late on Christmas Eve, Sir William Lyne agreed to resign as acting Prime Minister. And a relieved Lord Hopetoun instead appointed Sir Edmund Barton, who is now recognised as the first Prime Minister of Australia.

The lesson of this story? Don't make any big life decisions when you have typhoid fever. Also, democracy is a messy process. Also, sometimes prime ministers are like pancakes. The first one can turn out a bit wonky.

Poor old Lord Hopetoun didn't last long either. He served as Governor-General until 1902, at which point his request for a large personal expense account was refused by the Parliament, and he flounced back to Britain, where he died at just 47 years of age.

The White Australia Policy

The Australian people's desire for Federation was driven by a new sense of nationalism – of an emerging Australian identity that was different from Britain's. This sounds kind of nice and friendly, but there was a dark side. The huge influx of people from all over the world during the Gold Rush – particularly from China – had triggered hostility towards people from different cultures. One of the most popular arguments for Federation was that it would establish controls over who was allowed to move to Australia. The image promoted of an ideal Australia at the time was young, prosperous and white. In 1901, this racist approach was formalised as the *Immigration Restriction Act*, otherwise known as the White Australia Policy, which was widely supported across various political parties. It ruled that only white immigrants would be welcomed to the new nation of Australia.

In case you are reading this and thinking to yourself: 'Hey! This is a pretty rich attitude, isn't it, from a bunch of people who themselves arrived on boats and essentially pinched a giant landmass off the people who were already living there?' Well, the answer is: ***Yep. It was.***

Modern Australia is a nation built on immigration. Currently one-third of us were born overseas. And the only ones who have truly been here forever are First Nations people. Nonetheless, the White Australia Policy judged that white immigrants were more useful than non-white immigrants. This situation was in place for the first six decades of our life as a nation; it was partially dismantled by the Holt Government in 1966 and its last vestiges abolished by the Whitlam Government in 1973. And for much of that time, the **Commonwealth*** Parliament also took the view that white Australians should have full voting rights, but Aboriginal Australians shouldn't.

What can I say? History is full of acts and decisions that we look back upon today and think, 'That was wrong, and ignorant.' It's why studying history is important. And being honest about the past is important. As voters and citizens today, we can't change the mistakes of the past. But we can do the very best we can – as a democracy – to learn from them, to correct them where that's possible, and to ensure they aren't repeated.

A Day of Celebration

On 1 January 1901, the Commonwealth of Australia was proclaimed in Centennial Park, Sydney. There was a huge crowd. A grand procession. Celebrations that lasted more than a week. Sydney's Town Hall hosted a grand state dinner for 1000 attendees, which – in the words of one newspaper report – *'formed a fitting climax to a remarkable demonstration. Here were gathered a brilliant galaxy of the political and social intellectual stars of Australia.'*

Only men were invited to the grand banquet. Ladies were permitted to observe from the Town Hall's internal balconies though! And for all Australia's excitement about its proud new national identity, the evening's menu was entirely in French. The first dish listed – after an appetiser of local oysters – was *'Potage: Tortue Claire'*. Translation? A delicate soup of . . . turtle.

Hello, world! Presenting . . . the newly federated nation of Australia!

THE CONSTITUTION

There are many democracies in the world, and they're all a little bit different from each other – and in some cases, very different indeed! The word 'democracy' is derived from the Greek words 'demos' (people) and 'kratia' (power)... people power! Australia's is a representative democracy, which means that the people vote to elect representatives to make decisions on our behalf. But our system has other aspects as well – we're kind of like a pizza with the lot! For example, we are what's called a ***constitutional monarchy***, which means we have a monarch – currently King Charles – as our head of state. Even though they don't do very much at all apart from being a figurehead. We're also a Federation: a collection of states banded together into a nation.

When Australia's system was being designed, we borrowed bits and pieces from all over the place. We took the Lower House – the House of Representatives – from the British Parliament at Westminster. We also borrowed the Westminster tradition of having a prime minister. But we didn't adopt the British Upper House, which is called the House of Lords, and at the time was full of very posh aristocrats called things like Lord Cucumber Sandwich-Smythe the Third, who inherited their seats from their fathers. Instead, we borrowed the American Upper House – the Senate. It made more sense for us, seeing as like America we were going to be a collection of states. So we ended up with an artful mix of Westminster and Washington – some called it 'Washminster'.

And to make it official, a Constitution was written, to explain how the whole thing worked.

The Constitution is still the most important single document in Australia's system of government. Not that I'd say it's a ripping read, exactly. It *was* published in 1901, after all.

The Australian Constitution and founding documents, with Queen Victoria's signature and seal, are held at the National Archives of Australia just down the road from Parliament House. You can buy a nifty pocket-sized version in most newsagencies. There'll be a copy in your school library. And you can easily find it online.

Here's how it kicks off:

'Whereas the people of New South Wales, Victoria, South Australia, Queensland, and Tasmania, humbly relying on the blessing of Almighty God, have agreed to unite in one indissoluble Federal Commonwealth under the Crown of the United Kingdom of Great Britain and Ireland, and under the Constitution hereby established...'

You see what I mean? It doesn't exactly scream, ***'Read on, thrillseekers!'***

Despite the curly old-fashioned language, though, the Constitution remains incredibly powerful to this very day. It's been described as 'the birth certificate of the nation'. But it's *much* more important than that. A birth certificate just records where you were born, your embarrassing middle name, parents' names and what nationality you are. A birth certificate doesn't make rules for how you live your life, what your bedtime's going to be and whether it's absolutely definitely necessary for you to eat zucchini and so on.

Australia's Constitution, by contrast, does set rules. Many rules! It sets rules for how Australia is run. How the Parliament will work, how the court system will work and who's allowed to charge taxes. Most importantly, it sets rules about which areas of Australia are the responsibility of state governments, and which are the responsibility of the national – or federal, or Commonwealth – government.

And it's such a powerful document that when the Parliament makes a new law in Australia, it first has to check that the proposed law doesn't contradict anything in the Constitution. Sometimes – especially when parliamentary debates get complex and last-minute changes are made – things get messy! Over the course of our democratic history, governments have made many laws only to have them struck down because judges have found them to be in breach of the Constitution. The High Court of Australia – our most powerful court – is also found in Canberra. It has the ultimate say on whether a disputed law is consistent with the Constitution. If it's deemed inconsistent, the High Court has the power to strike the law down, which is a legal way of saying ***'Delete'***.

In order to wrap your head around any of this, you first need to understand what the Constitution is saying! There are a *lot* of lawyers – some of them sporting very fancy wigs – whose sole purpose and joy is to interpret the Constitution. It's a whole thing. Maybe it will become *your* thing? The ideas are quite fascinating, once you get into it.

So you can see that the Constitution is more like a strict instruction manual rather than a birth certificate. Governments absolutely have to follow its rules, even the ones they don't like.

'If the Constitution is so strict, why don't governments just change the Constitution?' you may ask.

Great question.

The answer is that the people who wrote the Constitution had already thought of this. So there is even a section in the Constitution that sets out what you have to do in order to change the Constitution.

It's very hard to pull off. You have to have a special national vote, called a referendum. Succeeding is so hard that out of 45 attempts to change the Constitution over the democratic history of Australia, it's only been done 8 times. You can find a simplified account of these referenda at the end of this chapter.

Looking at the questions that have been put to Australians over the years, you get a clear idea about the bits of the Constitution that Commonwealth governments found annoying. Some changes – like giving the Commonwealth more powers over industrial relations, or monopolies, or wanting to ensure Senate and House of Representatives elections are held on the same day – were put to the people several times with no success. Australians are cautious about giving governments more power, on the whole. The only referenda that have ever succeeded are ones where both the Government and the Opposition* are in favour.

Why Is It So Strict?

Like most questions around law and government and politics, the answer to this question is actually quite simple. ***Fear.*** A great motivator in politics! The main reason Federation took so long to come about was that the smaller states were afraid they'd get stomped all over by the bigger states. So the Constitution was written in a way that gives protection to the smaller states. Even if the most populous states of NSW and Victoria ganged up and tried to rewrite the Constitution, they wouldn't be able to do so.

And why does the Constitution still play such a huge role in how this country is governed, despite it being tricky to read and understand, and written over a century ago, even before planes were invented?

All our laws are based on the Constitution. Till this very day, if you want to change the Constitution, you have to get a hefty majority of the vote in a majority of the states and territories. That's very tricky to do.

WHAT CONSTITUTES THE CONSTITUTION?

The Australian Constitution is made up of 128 sections, gathered into 8 chapters. And seeing as the people who wrote it put such a huge amount of effort into constructing chapters, why don't we follow that structure for our brief and pleasant tour?

My version will be a whole lot simpler than the original document. So, if you're planning to become a constitutional lawyer, it might be worth reading some other versions as well. My version will probably only take you as far as high school.

The Parliament

The first chapter in the Constitution sets out the structure of the Australian Federal Parliament. It's pretty detailed, which is amazing given that it was written several decades before the Parliament even got its own building! It's here where the elements of design, as argued by the delegates to the Constitutional conventions,

> ***A convention is an unwritten rule, an accepted practice that has been built up over a long time (sometimes centuries!). It's not a law. The Australian Constitution is a combination of literal interpretation and convention.***

are spelled out. Such as the role of the Governor-General – the representative of the British monarch – who is the final step for signing laws into existence. And the two chambers – the House of Representatives and the Senate. The Constitution goes into great detail about how these houses operate, what happens when senators or members disagree, or die, and whether someone is allowed to be a member of both houses at once. ***(Spoiler alert: No.)***

More importantly, there is a bit (in Section 51) that sets out where the Parliament of Australia has specific power to make laws. Basically, it picks out the areas that will be the responsibility of the federal Parliament. As you read the list, think about the people who composed it, more than a century ago.

As the new nation was designed, there were all sorts of arguments about which responsibilities the colonies would hold on to, and which they'd hand over to the new national parliament. Some of the nominated issues were very obviously national matters, especially for an island nation. Immigration, for instance. Defence. Trade with other countries. Quarantine. Fisheries. Pensions.

Others were aspects of life where it just made sense for everyone to follow the same rules. So, the Commonwealth also took over responsibility for currency – the coins or notes we use. The laws governing marriage. Communication, which in those days meant the postal service, telegraph wires and so on. Disputes about wages in national industries. Weights and measures. Naturalisation and aliens. Lighthouses. Railway lines. ***(Finally!)***

Ask your teacher what coins and notes are!

'Aliens' doesn't mean creatures from another planet. It's an early term for immigrants, and we have always had lots of those.

In 1901, this list of Commonwealth responsibilities was considered comprehensive. What else could a new government possibly need?

The Executive Government

The party or group with the most elected members in the House of Representatives is the party that ends up forming the Government. And up to 30 of those Members of Parliament then become ministers, each with a special responsibility. You see ministers in the media all the time. The Minister for Health standing in front of a health clinic, the Minister for Defence crawling about on a tank, the Minister for Education standing in front of a university. Each of them commands a department of staff (called public servants) working to run public services like hospitals, the army, universities and the like. Ministers are collectively called the 'Executive' and they have their own wing in Parliament House. They report to the Prime Minister. And Chapter 2 of the Constitution is full of rules about how much they are paid, how many of them there can be, who they're allowed to boss around and so on.

Blue carpet, remember?

Do you know who isn't actually mentioned anywhere in the Constitution? ***THE PRIME MINISTER!*** Weird, huh? Australia's political parties weren't mentioned in the Constitution either – mainly because they weren't invented yet. But an amendment in 1977 mentioned parties for the first time.

The Prime Minister seems like a more serious omission! But the design of the House of Representatives was closely modelled on the British House of Commons. The idea of a ***'prime'*** minister was so obvious at the time that it didn't get an explicit mention.

Here's another convention: under the terms of the Constitution, ministers are appointed solely by the Governor-General. But in practice, the list of ministers is handed to the Governor-General by the Prime Minister, whose decision it really is. Even though the Prime Minister isn't actually mentioned. All clear? Terrific. Welcome to constitutional law! Sometimes, it is full of mysteries. Also, wigs.

The Judicature

This is just a fancy name for courts. One of the great challenges of designing a democracy is installing lots of protections. This means lots of rules, and lots of consequences for breaking the rules so that people don't get elected into Government and then decide they're going to rip up the rulebook and declare themselves Special Forever Lord High God Thing and put everybody's taxes into their own giant piggy bank and so on.

Chapter 3 of the Constitution sets up the most powerful court in the land, the High Court, to enforce the rules. The High Court has the power to overturn any law the federal Parliament makes if that law breaks any of the rules of the Constitution.

Yes, this has happened many times. And it always makes prime ministers grumpy when it happens. But the rules are the rules, and part of a working democracy is that you follow the rules, even when they make you grumpy.

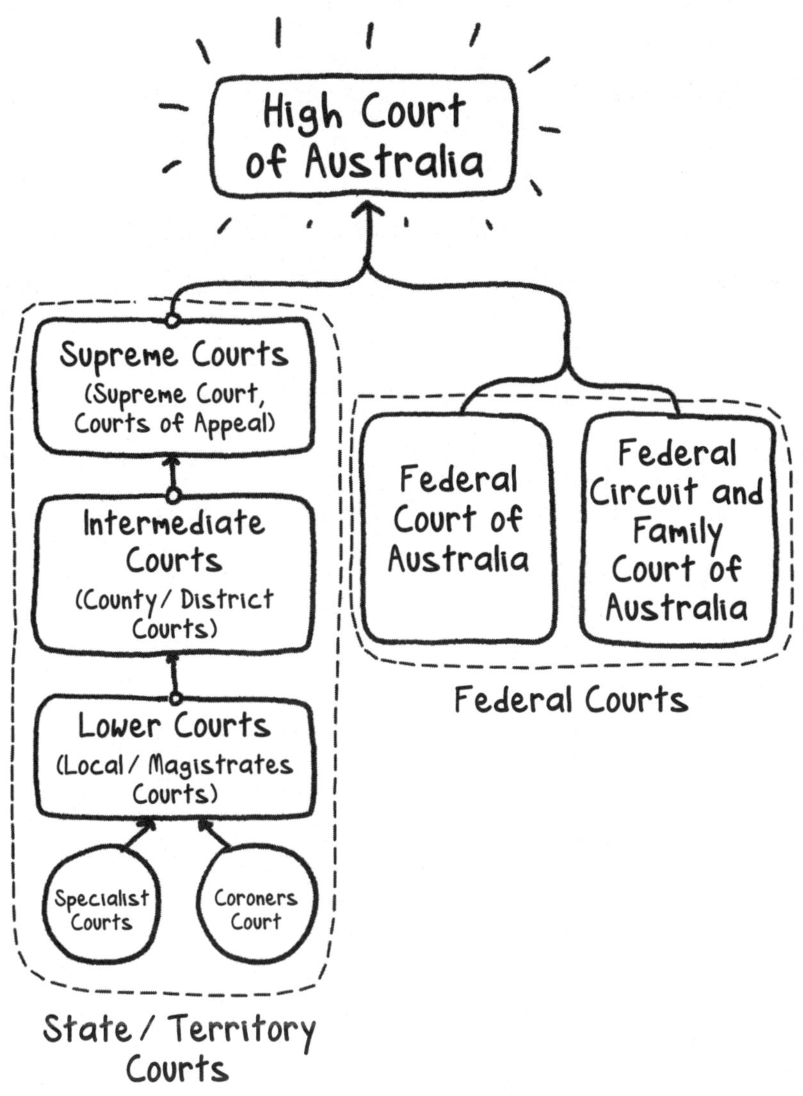

If you're planning to be a High Court judge, keep in mind that Section 72 decrees that you have to be younger than 70 years old to serve. So get cracking! This is not like the United States of America where you can be a judge on the Supreme Court for as long as you fancy the work. The oldest ever American Supreme Court judge was Oliver Wendell Holmes Jr, who retired in 1932 at age 90, having served on the court for 29 years. Yikes!

Finance and Trade

Chapter 4 was very important at the time of writing the Constitution. When six different colonies decide to form a nation, some of the most complicated – and hotly disputed – questions will be around money. How to make it? Who can spend it?

Governments can't provide services (hospitals, schools, jails and all the other government-funded things around us) unless they raise money to pay for them. And the main way for a government to raise money is by a system called taxation.

Broadly speaking, there are two systems of taxation. One type is on earnings – citizens pay a proportion of their income to a government in tax, and it's called income tax. Or companies pay a tax on their profits, and that's called company tax. The other kind of tax is an 'excise', where governments add a little bit to the price of goods that are bought and sold. Excise is charged on things like fuel and alcohol. Also, Australia has something called a GST – Goods and Services Tax – that is charged on lots of things that Australians buy, from toys to haircuts.

At the time of Federation, you could safely describe the range of taxation systems in place across the colonies as 'hectic'.

Some of the colonies had an income tax. Some had special taxes to pay for specific things. Lots of them charged excises on goods bought and sold from other colonies.

So, this section of the Constitution decrees that there must be free trade between all the states. The states could no longer charge excises on goods being bought and sold across state lines. Under this section, the new Commonwealth Government of Australia would take on responsibility for international trade, and the capacity to raise certain taxes. But there are a whole lot of protections for states in there too, again mostly so the smaller states didn't find themselves the victims of a tax grab from a bigger state.

It was a pretty good attempt to eliminate future disputes, but it's my sorry duty to report that even more than a century later, bickering about tax between the Commonwealth Government and the states is still a very big part of politics.

The States

Get your wigs ready, constitutional lawyers, because Chapter 5 of the Constitution raises a lot more questions than it answers.

As Constitutional chapters go, this one is not super long. Heaps of it is designed to reassure nervous colonial leaders signing up to Federation.

First, it garbles on for a few sections about how just because there is a new Commonwealth Government, it doesn't mean that the states and colonies are erased, and the laws of the colonies continue to be laws and so on.

There are additional calming sections for the existing colonial governments (like Section 119, which guarantees the Commonwealth will defend any state that comes under attack), and calming ones for the new Commonwealth too (like Section 114, which says the states are *not* allowed to start their own armies). ***Phew.***

Chapter 5 has some inclusions that immediately make you picture the person who demanded it. Like Section 113, 'Intoxicating Liquids', which is clear that states are allowed to make their own laws about alcohol even if that alcohol is made in another state. I picture a *very* red-faced colonial chap insisting that this section be included.

The most significant section of this chapter is Section 109. It says that in cases where a Commonwealth law and a state law contradict each other, the Commonwealth law wins. Section 109 is like a constitutional game of Scissors, Paper, Rock. And it has been an exciting section for constitutional scholars and lawyers over the years. Why? Well, because there have been many instances where the laws made by state governments clash with the laws made by the Commonwealth Government. And while Section 109 sounds simple – Rock beats Scissors, Commonwealth wins – the reality is more complicated. What if a state law only *partially* contradicts the Commonwealth law? What if one government thinks there's a contradiction and the other government doesn't? What if the law is about an area that the Constitution doesn't mention? How do you then decide whether that area is a state or Commonwealth responsibility?

This is where the court system comes in handy. The High Court is specifically charged with handling major questions of Constitutional interpretation. So, finding the answers to these sticky questions usually means lots and ***lots*** of lawyers.

One thing that makes these questions more difficult, of course, is that more than a century has elapsed since the Constitution was written. And while that list of areas where the Commonwealth is in charge made pretty good sense in 1901 (for example, lighthouses, money, defence, immigration, railways and telegraph systems), there have been a lot of areas for lawmaking that have developed since, which were not even imaginable in 1901.

Who's Responsible for Laws About the Internet?

Lawyers have to interpret the Constitution in terms of the intention of the people who wrote and approved it. So, on the internet, it's reasonable to assume that when the authors of the Constitution decided that national communications systems like telephones and telegrams and the Post Office should be governed nationally, they probably also meant to include 'any other national forms of communication that haven't been invented yet'.

The first Constitutional case the High Court heard happened in 1904, when the Commonwealth was only three years old. It was brought by a man called Henry D'Emden, who was the Deputy Postmaster-General of Tasmania. He was paid by the Commonwealth Government to do that job, but he got arrested by the Superintendent of Police in Tasmania because he didn't pay the Tasmanian **stamp duty*** on his payslip. D'Emden argued that because he was a Commonwealth employee he didn't have to pay state taxes on his income. Broadly, the High Court agreed with him.

(Section 51 says post offices are a Commonwealth responsibility, remember?)

Many more amusing variations on this case were to come, including one later in 1904 where the High Court had to decide whether Alfred Deakin (Australia's second Prime Minister) had to pay income tax in his home state of Victoria. It was an amazing time to be a lawyer.

New States

Chapter 6 of the Constitution reassures states that they can't be eliminated by the Commonwealth using a special Constitutional ray gun or anything. It hasn't been too controversial.

Miscellaneous

'Miscellaneous' is a terrific word. Constitutionally, its rough translation is 'things that didn't quite fit into the other chapters and we are all *very* tired here now at the Constitutional Convention so we are going to put all of them into one wonky chapter like Christmas leftovers'.

There were only three sections in Chapter 7 when it was finally agreed: Sections 125, 126 and 127.

Section 125 concerned the location of the new national parliament – the 'Seat of Government'. Nobody could agree where that would be, so Section 125 just says that the Seat of Government shall be somewhere in NSW but it has to be more than 100 miles (160 kilometres) from Sydney, and also it needs to be a patch of land more than 100 square miles

(259 square kilometres) in size, and also it has to be given for free if possible, and until then the Parliament will sit in Melbourne but this is absolutely not a permanent arrangement.

Just reading this section makes me feel tired.

Section 126 says that the Queen (that would be Queen Victoria) has the power to authorise the Governor-General to appoint deputies.

Section 127 has since been abolished (removed). But as legislated in 1901, it read: *'In reckoning the numbers of the people of the Commonwealth, or of a State or other part of the Commonwealth, aboriginal natives shall not be counted.'*

What this meant was that when calculating the number of people in a state in order to calculate Commonwealth payments or the size of electorates and so on, First Nations people simply were not counted. This section was legislated in 1901. It was not abolished until the Constitutional referendum of 1967 – one of the few that succeeded.

Alteration of the Constitution

When laws are made in the federal Parliament in Canberra (an exciting process, to be covered in chapters to come), one of the important questions that has to be answered first is, 'Does this law go against anything in the Constitution?' Even though the Constitution is more than a century old, this document still runs the show in Australia.

Chapter 8 details what needs to happen to change the Constitution. Both Houses of Parliament have to approve a piece of legislation spelling out the exact proposed changes, and then those changes have to be put to every single voter in Australia in a special vote called a referendum. The proposed new wording is printed on a ballot paper and voters have to mark either ***'Yes'*** or ***'No'***. The change will only be made if a majority of voters nationally vote 'Yes', *and* a majority of states have a 'Yes' vote over 50 per cent.

DOUBLE MAJORITY

The Australian Constitution can only be changed with the support of the majority of Australian voters AND a majority of voters in a majority of states (i.e. at least 4 states).

*Votes from the ACT, NT and other territories are ONLY counted in the national majority.

Every Referendum in Australia Ever

Here are my simplifications of the 45 Constitutional reform attempts that have been made over the life of our Federation.

Only eight have managed to secure both a national majority of 'Yes' votes *and* a majority in a majority of states. Eight out of 45! This is not a strike rate that would get you picked for the Australian cricket team.

1906	Should we change Senate terms to start on 1 July instead of 1 January?	✓ YES!
1910	Should the Commonwealth Government have the power to take over state debts?	✓ YES!
	Should we extend the Commonwealth's financial powers over the states?	✗ NO!
1911	Should we extend the Commonwealth's trade and commerce powers?	✗ NO!
	Should we give the Commonwealth new powers to nationalise monopoly businesses?	✗ NO!
1913	Should we extend the Commonwealth's trade and commerce powers?	✗ STILL NO!
	Should we give the Commonwealth more powers over corporations?	✗ NO!

Should we give the Commonwealth more powers over industrial matters? ✗ NO!

Should we give the Commonwealth new powers over trusts? ✗ NO!

Should we give the Commonwealth powers over monopoly businesses? ✗ STILL NO!

Should we give the Commonwealth powers over state industrial matters in the railway sector? ✗ NO!

1919 Should we give the Commonwealth more powers over trade, corporations, industrial affairs and trusts? ✗ STOP ASKING THESE QUESTIONS IN CRAFTY NEW WAYS, THE ANSWER IS STILL NO!

Should we give the Commonwealth new powers over monopoly businesses? ✗ UGH. FOR THE THIRD TIME: NO!

1926 Hey guys. Just wondering, do you reckon we should give the Commonwealth more powers over corporations and trusts? ✗ HARD STARE. NO!

What about if we gave the Commonwealth the power to intervene and maintain essential services to protect the public in the event of an emergency? ✗ ALSO, NO!

1928 The Commonwealth and the states have made an agreement giving the Commonwealth a little bit more power over state debts, in return for some sweet cash. Okay if that goes into the Constitution? ✓ YES!

1937	Should we give the Commonwealth powers over aviation and planes, seeing as how they have now been invented?	✗ NO!
	Can the Commonwealth have specific powers to run agricultural marketing schemes like the national quota for dried fruit?	✗ WAIT, WHAT? ACTUALLY, JUST NO!
1944	Is it okay if the Commonwealth holds on to all these fancy new powers it took over in World War Two, just for another five years?	✗ NO!
1946	You know how the Commonwealth has responsibility for aged and invalid pensions? What about if we added maternity allowances, unemployment benefits and some others?	✓ YES!
	Great! Also what about that dried fruit thing from 1937? Could we do that?	✗ STILL NO!
	Shall we give the Commonwealth powers over employment in industry?	✗ NO!
1948	Should we give the Commonwealth powers over rents and prices?	✗ NO!
1951	Should we give the Commonwealth specific powers to smash communism?	✗ NO!
1967	Can we increase the number of MPs in the House of Representatives without also increasing the number of Senators?	✗ NO!

	Shall we give the Commonwealth specific powers to make laws for Aboriginal people, and also should Aboriginal people be counted in the population for electoral purposes?	✓ YES!
	Shall we give the Commonwealth power over prices?	✗ NO!
	What about over incomes?	✗ ABSOLUTELY NOT. NO.
1974	Shall we change the Constitution to ensure that elections for the House of Representatives and for the Senate are held at the same time?	✗ NO!
	Shall we make it easier to change the Constitution?	✗ NO!
	Shall we calculate electorate boundaries based on population, rather than number of eligible voters?	✗ NO!
	Should the Commonwealth be able to borrow money on behalf of local governments?	✗ NO!
1977	Seriously though, shouldn't it be the rule that Senate and House of Representatives elections happen at the same time?	✗ STILL NO!
	Should it be the rule that when a Senator dies or leaves between elections they should be replaced by a person from the same party?	✓ YES!

1977	Should Territorians get a vote in referenda?	✓ YES!
	Should we make federal judges retire at 70?	✓ YES!
1984	About elections for the Senate and the House of Representatives. Same time?	✗ NO!
	Should we make it so that the Commonwealth and states can agree to transfer powers between them?	✗ NO!
1988	Should we have fixed four-year electoral terms?	✗ NO!
	Should we change the electoral rules so that every vote has the same value?	✗ NO!
	Should we put local government in the Constitution?	✗ NO!
	What about a statement of some basic human rights?	✗ NO!
1999	Should we become a republic?	✗ NO!
	Should we insert a preamble in the Constitution recognising First Nations people?	✗ NO!
2023	Should there be a special advisory council called The Voice to advocate directly to Parliament for First Nations people?	✗ NO!

Referendum or Plebiscite?

When Australians are called upon to vote on a special issue, it's not always called a referendum. A referendum is a vote to change the Constitution, and it must follow precisely all the steps laid out in this chapter. It's compulsory to vote in a referendum. But over the life of our Federation, there have been some occasions on which we've had a national vote that wasn't about changing the Constitution, and wasn't compulsory. These are called 'plebiscites'.

Like in 1916 and 1917, when Australians were asked by Prime Minister Billy Hughes to support 'conscription' - which would force young men to go to war. The nation voted 'No'. Twice.

Or in 1977, when Australians were asked to choose our national anthem. The choices were 'God Save the Queen', 'Waltzing Matilda', 'Advance Australia Fair' or a ditty called 'Song of Australia', which had won a special contest in South Australia. South Australia voted for that one, but everyone else went for 'Advance Australia Fair'.

In 2017, Australians were asked to vote on whether same-sex couples should be allowed to get married. It wasn't a referendum, because it didn't involve a change to the Constitution. The Government of the day called it a 'postal survey'. Was it actually a plebiscite? Ah, yep. It was. But we called it a 'postal survey'. Because...I don't know. REASONS.

In 2023, the Labor Government led by Anthony Albanese held a referendum to propose the creation of a special advisory council called the Voice to Parliament, designed to give First Nations people a direct input into policy decisions. The proposal came from a long consultation process that began in 2015, supported jointly by then-Prime Minister Malcolm Turnbull and Opposition leader Bill Shorten. A special First Nations Constitutional Convention occurred in 2017, where Aboriginal leaders discussed and debated how Australia's Constitution could be changed to recognise and better serve the continent's original Traditional Owners. It produced the iconic Uluru Statement From the Heart, which you can read in full at www.ulurustatement.org

The Convention agreed that policy about Aboriginal people in Australia was too often made by governments without consulting them properly. And so the Voice to Parliament was proposed. Anthony Albanese pledged to hold the Voice referendum as his first priority when he won the 2022 federal election. But the Opposition, led by the Liberal Party's Peter Dutton, opposed the idea of the Voice to Parliament. The referendum was defeated, and the recognition of Indigenous Australians in the Australian Constitution remains unresolved.

CONSTITUTIONAL CRISES!

The Constitution can trip politicians up in unexpected ways, too.

There's a bit in Section 44 of Chapter 1 that says people are ineligible to sit in the Parliament if they are '*under any acknowledgement of allegiance, obedience, or adherence to a foreign power*' or are '*a subject or a citizen of a foreign power*'.

The Constitution doesn't say you have to be an Australian citizen to be eligible to sit in Parliament. How could it? The Constitution came into effect in 1901 and Australian citizenship didn't even become a thing until 1949. So, everyone has just assumed that Section 44 means parliamentarians aren't allowed to be dual citizens or citizens of another nation.

The thing is, running for Parliament is a very busy and distracting job and sometimes candidates forget to check if they have any other citizenships knocking around. Sometimes, they can automatically be a citizen of another country and not know about it.

In June 2017, a lawyer in Perth called John Cameron, who happened to be interested in the citizenship of federal MPs, ran a check on the New Zealand citizenship register and discovered that the Western Australian Greens Senator Scott Ludlam was actually a New Zealand citizen as well as an Australian citizen. Senator Ludlam resigned. His colleague Larissa Waters – a Greens Senator from Queensland – quickly checked her own status and found that she had Canadian citizenship. ***Whoops!*** She resigned too. Then the Queensland Liberal National Party Senator Matt Canavan discovered to his horror that his mum – an Italian and Australian citizen – had signed him up for Italian citizenship when he was in his twenties but forgot to tell him about it. Soon, every Member of Parliament was panicking about their own status and referring themself to the High Court for assessment and by the end of the panic 15 of them had either resigned or been declared ineligible to sit in the Parliament.

This series of debacles was described as a '*constitutional crisis*' but it's not the biggest constitutional crisis in our history. That one happened in 1975.

In 1972, after 23 years of Liberal Party rule, Australia elected the Labor Government of Gough Whitlam. The new Government made a lot of major changes, many of which were vehemently opposed by the Liberals. The Government called a **double dissolution*** election in 1974 to get some of its changes through, and won. But in late 1975, the Opposition refused to pass legislation through the Senate approving money for the Government to govern. This is called 'blocking supply' and it's quite unusual. Prime Minister Whitlam went to the Governor-General (who had a lot of formal power under the Constitution as the representative of the monarch) to ask for another election. The Governor-General, Sir John Kerr, refused to grant

Section 61 of the Constitution says executive power is given to the monarch and delegated to the Governor-General. This means the Governor-General is a part of both the Parliament and the Government, and carries out tasks on behalf of the Monarch.

an election and instead sacked the Prime Minister, and invited the Opposition leader Malcolm Fraser to form a government instead. Malcolm Fraser did, then called another election, which the Liberals won. It was the end of the Whitlam Government. This event is referred to as **the Dismissal.***

This caused a huge kerfuffle. In practice, the Governor-General follows the advice of the Prime Minister. Under the Constitution, the Governor-General does have some rather sweeping powers. Including the power to, er, ***sack*** the Prime Minister. And that's what happened, to Mr Whitlam's dismay.

BLERP!! BLERP!! BLERP!!
Convention Alert!!
Convention Alert!!
Warning!! Conventions Can Be Ignored!!
BLERP!! BLERP!! BLERP!!

Sir John Kerr's decision remains a highly controversial one to this day. It was a demonstration that where the Constitution is concerned, you can't rely on convention.

4

WHY DO WE VOTE?

When an adult Australian citizen walks into a voting booth on federal Election Day, we have our names marked off the roll and are handed two bits of paper. One will be green and small and list about 6–10 names. The other will be white and often very long, usually the size of a bed sheet, and lists many, many more names.

Why do we fill out two separate voting papers? Because our Parliament is made up of two chambers (bicameral parliament): the House of Representatives (or Lower House) and the Senate (or Upper House). The two Houses of Parliament are elected separately. Hence, two bits of paper. The way we vote on these two bits of paper will help to elect 226 politicians in total to represent us in Canberra. Let's look at the ballot papers, one by one.

THE HOUSE OF REPRESENTATIVES: THE GREEN BALLOT

Australia is divided up into 150 chunks, called ***electorates***. The average number of voters in one electorate is around 120,000, though there is some variation due to population density. At the 2025 federal election, the electorate with the fewest voters was teensy-weensy Clark, in Tasmania, which had 74,315 voters – only half the headcount of the Queensland seat of Longman, with 142,810. But mostly, we try to keep them around the same size. And on Election Day, each area elects one representative called a Member of Parliament (or MP).

When Parliament sits (on average 18–20 weeks a year), all 150 of these representatives come from around Australia to meet in the big room in Canberra called the House of Representatives Chamber. You might remember from our tour around Parliament House in the first chapter of this book that this chamber has green carpet, and enough green leather seats for everyone. Sometimes, electorates are called 'seats', even though they'd be hard to sit on. That's because each one literally translates to a seat in the House of Representatives.

Our chambers are designed to look like the British House of Commons – the Government and the Opposition sit on opposite sides, with a big desk running down the middle. The Prime Minister and Opposition leader sit at the desk on opposite sides. When they get up to ask or answer questions, they stand at the 'Despatch Boxes' on either side of the big desk. The big desk is wide enough so that the opposing sides are ***two swords' width apart***. This dates back to the old days where parliamentarians still had swords. The distance was measured so the two sides could argue safely without losing their tempers and slashing each other. This isn't an issue anymore, but it's a clue as to why sometimes Parliament gets loud and shouty.

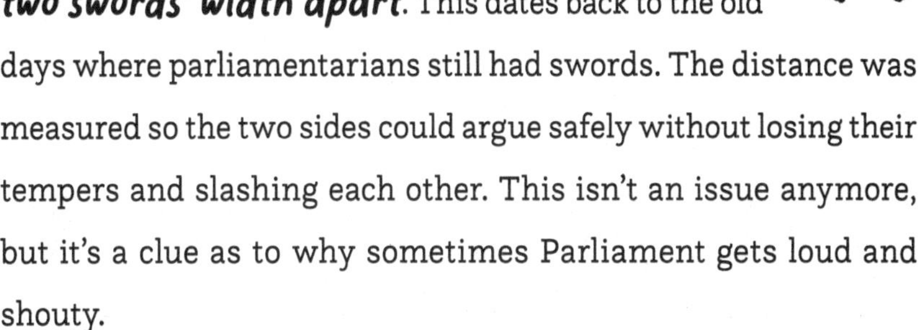

Australia borrowed and adapted the colour from the British House of Commons, too. The green used in the House of Representatives is representative of the grey-green colours of the Australian landscape.

HOUSE OF REPRESENTATIVES

Lower House

Opposition side

6

5

7

15

Key

1. Speaker of the House
2. **Clerk of the House***
3. Clerk's friend
4. Government front bench
5. Opposition front bench
6. Press Gallery
7. Opposition backbench
8. Despatch Box
9. Weirdy hourglasses
10. Prime Minister
11. **Mace***
12. Leader of the Opposition
13. Hansard person
14. Government **backbenchers***
15. Crossbench

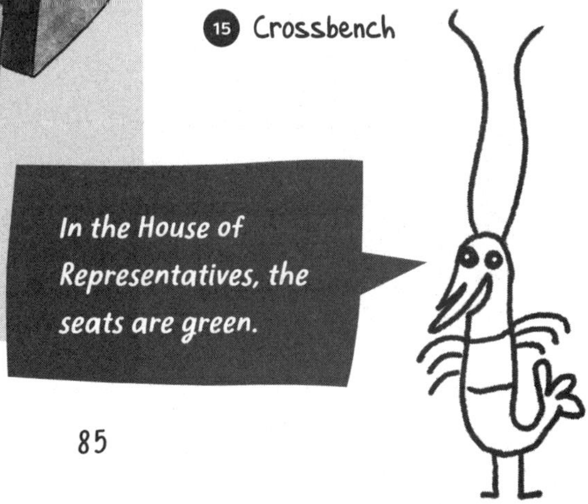

In the House of Representatives, the seats are green.

Key

1. Coat of Arms
2. Party logos
3. Boxes to put your numbers in
4. Signature of electoral officer
5. Candidate surname (and given names)
6. Party name

House of Representatives ballots are always GREEN. But this book is black-and-white, so you will just have to imagine it!

The green House of Representatives voting paper you get handed when you walk into the voting station has a list of names with boxes next to them. They are the names of the candidates – that's what we call the people who have put their hand up to be the member for the electorate you live in. In the Australian system of voting, which is called ***'preferential voting'***, you have to put a number in every box, ranking the candidates in your order of preference. So if there are six candidates, you put a '1' next to the person you like the most, a '2' next to the person you like second-best, all the way through to number 6, which is what you put next to the name of the person you think is absolutely the biggest wally of all the options presented.

Preferential Voting

Of all the things that make the Australian voting system unusual, this is the biggie – we have preferential voting. We're the only nation in the world to use it so enthusiastically and thoroughly as a national standard. In Britain, for instance, they use a much simpler system called 'First past the post'. It's a bit misleading because there isn't actually a post! If you have six candidates in a 'first past the post' system, all it means is that each voter votes for just one candidate, and the candidate with the highest number of votes wins.

What's good about this British system? ***SIMPLICITY!*** Easy to count.

What's bad about this system? ***GRUMPY VOTERS!*** Because – if opinion is evenly divided – the candidate with the most votes might not actually get anywhere near 50 per cent of the vote. And that means more voters will be disappointed than happy.

Here's how our preferential voting works. Each voter numbers their preferred candidates, let's say from one to eight. In the vote count, the ballot papers are sorted into eight piles, according to which candidate has scored the number 1 preference. If someone has more than 50 per cent of all the votes, it's simple – they win! If no one has more than half of all the votes, then things get a bit more complicated. The candidate who has the smallest pile (the lowest number of number 1 votes) is eliminated. Their pile gets 'distributed', meaning all those ballot papers are now added to the pile of whoever it is who got the number 2 on each of those ballots. And then the next candidate with the least total votes gets eliminated. And their pile gets distributed. And so on, until a candidate reaches more than 50 per cent. And that candidate will be elected.

In this way, Australian voters get to pick not only their favourite candidate, but their second-favourite, and third, and so on. The idea is that even if you don't get your dream result, you at least get a say in your next preference, which lessens the chance of getting your absolute nightmare.

Charles Dodgson was an eccentric mathematician who lived and taught at Oxford University. He also had an incredibly famous literary alter ego – under the name Lewis Carroll, he wrote many books including *Alice in Wonderland*, and dreamed up the most remarkable inventions. A contraption for taking notes in the dark. A steering device for a long-forgotten Victorian type of tricycle. He even invented an early version of Scrabble!

But Dodgson's major obsession was with fairness. He designed a fairer way to run the Wimbledon tennis tournament. It wasn't adopted. And he spent a lot of time tinkering with a design for a voting system that was fairer than Britain's 'first past the post' model. He came up with a system for preferential voting and had a pamphlet printed, which he enthusiastically distributed to British parliamentarians in 1884. Sadly, nobody was very interested in Dodgson's fairer voting model. He died in 1898, so he never knew that on the other side of the world, in Australia – a country in which Alice fears she might end up if she falls too far down the rabbit hole – we adopted preferential voting in 1918, 20 years after his death. Our model is based on the work of other mathematicians, but the principle is the same: if you ask voters to rank their preferences, you end up electing a compromise candidate who is the one more people can live with.

Back to the voting booth, with its green paper and its list of candidates. Now, I hear what you're saying. 'How do I know which of all these candidates I like the first, second or sixth best? Am I supposed to have met them all?'

Here's where we need to take a quick break for a word about political parties. Most of the names on that ballot paper will be the names of people representing a political party, and that helps voters understand what exactly they're voting for. Candidates who choose to join a political party generally align with the same values of the party.

On most ballot papers in Australian elections, you'll see a candidate from the Liberal Party, a candidate from the Australian Labor Party, and a candidate from the Greens. In country areas, there will also usually be a candidate from the National Party.

These are the established parties in Australia, but you'll also see other types of candidates from parties that try to appeal to people who feel passionate about a particular subject. The Shooters, Fishers and Farmers Party, for instance, has candidates who tend to have a special interest in gun laws, or the laws around fishing. There are also parties that are grouped around a particular leader, like Pauline Hanson's One Nation, Bob Katter's Australia Party or the Jacqui Lambie Network.

Likewise in the early 2000s, there was a No Pokies Party, which was formed to campaign against the spread of gaming machines.

Sometimes there are even joke parties. The Deadly Serious Party existed in Australia during the 1980s. The DSP's main defence policy was a plan to dispatch a flock of killer penguins to protect Australia's coastline. Sadly, the Deadly Serious Party was deregistered on 2 November 1988 for not having the required minimum of 500 members. Possibly because penguins don't vote.

Similarly, the Sun Ripened Warm Tomato Party, formed in the ACT in 1989, experienced only a short burst of significance, disappearing soon after. It's sorely missed, especially by voters with crusty bread and olive oil.

You'll also see other candidates who describe themselves as Independent. This means they're not a member of any political party. They're seeking to represent the local area under their own steam.

Historically, the majority of voters in Australia choose either Liberal or Labor when voting for the House of Representatives. And this is important, because the House of Representatives is where it's decided which party has won the election, which party is going to become the Government, and therefore – very crucially – which party leader becomes ***Prime Minister of Australia***.

The Coalition*

The Liberal Party is the traditional main opponent of the Labor Party in Australia's political system, but you'll often hear the term 'Coalition' used to describe a Liberal government. How come? Because the Liberal Party almost always teams up with the National Party, which is the party that pitches itself as the representative of country people and farmers. They sign a special agreement called the 'Coalition agreement' where their MPs agree to vote together, and their numbers are counted together when calculating which party has won the most seats. 'Coalition' is a fancy word for 'team'. And the first Coalition government, comprised of MPs from what was back then called the Country Party, added to what was then called the Nationalist Party, was forged in a deal after the 1922 election.

The Country Party is now known as the National Party, and the Nationalist Party's modern equivalent is the Liberal Party. But the idea of country conservatives banding together with their suburban conservative cousins is still a very current thing. They do tend to argue a lot, though. And they've split up a few times, most recently for eight whole days after the 2025 election, due to some disagreements over climate change and nuclear power. But let's not get distracted! Back to the election!

After the voting booths close at 6 pm, the counting starts. In each of the 150 electorates, the votes are carefully tallied up to work out which candidate has the most votes, and therefore who has been elected in that seat.

The count is very important and serious, so it's undertaken by special representatives of an independent organisation called the Australian Electoral Commission. The AEC is in charge of registering people to vote, making sure they only vote once, and then counting the votes very carefully. Australia believes it's important to have someone independent in charge of this process. We don't want – for example – to ask the Labor Party secretary or the Liberal Party director to be in charge of the count. We could never be quite sure that a person like that wouldn't just be all, 'Oh yeah so I counted the votes, and it turns out we won by a total landslide, yay us!'

The AEC carries out the count under observation from representatives of the parties (called scrutineers) who keep an eagle eye on things to make sure no votes are missed or counted the wrong way.

Do disputes occur? They sure do. Sometimes voters get mixed up and do ticks or crosses instead of writing numbers on the ballot paper. Sometimes they write messages or draw little doodles. And then everyone in the count argues about what they meant, and whether this doodle means a vote for this person or that person. Mostly, the doodle votes don't get assigned to a party. They're deemed to be **'informal' votes,*** which means that they don't count at all. To be valid, a ballot paper needs to show the voter's clear intention. These are called **'formal' votes.*** So long as a clear and complete order of preference is shown, the AEC will accept numbers, words (one, two, three), letters (A, B, C) and even Roman numerals! AEC officials always keep a chart of Roman numerals somewhere close by, because there really are voters who like to use them.

On the night of the election, as soon as voting closes at 6 pm, at every voting station (they're also called 'booths') around the country, the AEC officials count the votes they've collected and phone the results through to enter into the AEC's centralised computer system. They work fast, because everyone wants to know as quickly as possible who has won.

The AEC publishes results on its website as they come in, and as the hours roll by and more and more of the total vote has been counted, we can see which candidates have been elected.

This is just the first very fast count, by the way. The AEC officials will do another slower count in the following days, once they've collected all the ballot papers together for each electorate. Counts that are very close may be subjected to a recount. The AEC is very thorough.

But on the night, as each individual seat is won by the Liberal Party or the Labor Party, it's added to their pile, and as soon as a major party has won more than half of the seats in the Parliament – that is, 76 or more – then it becomes clear that that party is going to form the Government. And the leader of that party will be the Prime Minister.

A REMINDER! In Australia, we don't vote personally for the Prime Minister, unless we happen to be in their electorate. We're not like America, where they have a President who is directly elected. Remember – Australia copied our Lower House from the British system. We choose between candidates from various parties, and the leader of the party with the majority of seats becomes the Prime Minister.

Once the result has become clear, generally late on election night, the leader of the losing party calls the leader of the winning party to 'concede'.

This means saying, 'Well done, you won, I wish you all the best, democracy is the winner tonight,' even if they're incredibly annoyed.

More on this job later.

The leader of the losing party becomes the Leader of the Opposition.

On the evening of the election, the major political parties each hold a big event where everyone stands around watching the election broadcast. Once the result's clear, the leader of the losing party comes out and gives a big speech about how it's been a tough night but they'll try again in three years. The leader of the winning party will then show up on stage at their election event and everyone goes ***berserk***.

If the leader has kids, they will almost certainly have to stand up awkwardly on stage wearing unusually smart clothing for midnight on a Saturday. It is not easy to be the child of a famous politician. It's like being the child of a teacher at your school, times one million. If you ever meet one of these children, please be nice to them!

On a few occasions in Australian political history, neither major party has got to 76 seats. This is called a **hung parliament*** and it usually happens when the major parties get a roughly equal number of seats. In this situation, the rest of the seats are held by Independents or minor party representatives so no one can automatically become the Government. What happens then is a round of negotiations where both major parties try to persuade a few of the people who were elected either as Independents or minor party representatives into supporting them to become the Government.

In 2010, the federal election officially yielded a hung parliament. Australia's first female Prime Minister, Julia Gillard (leader of the Labor Party), successfully persuaded a handful of Independents and a Greens candidate to support her rather than Tony Abbott, the leader of the Liberal Party. This process of negotiation took ***19 days!***

These negotiations can be about anything. In 2002, in the state election in South Australia, when the result was a hung parliament, the Labor Party eventually managed to form a government after promising an Independent called Peter Lewis that they would phase out commercial river fishing in his electorate, and get rid of a weed called branched broomrape, which had been getting on Mr Lewis's nerves. When Julia Gillard negotiated to reach the deal in 2010, the detail was a bit more complicated (such as promising a package of parliamentary reforms) but a bit less exotic.

THE SENATE: THE BIG VOTING PAPER

The Senate is the other chamber of Parliament House. Also called the Upper House, it's about a 100-metre stroll away from the House of Representatives chamber, and has red carpet and red seats, just so that nobody ever gets **confused** and turns up to vote in the wrong chamber. There are only 76 Senators, so it's about half the size of the House of Representatives.

We borrowed the red from the British parliament (House of Lords). Australian Parliament House colours have been adapted – the red in the Senate is reflective of the red ochre in the Australian landscape.

The significant thing about the Senate is that it's elected in a totally different way from the House of Representatives.

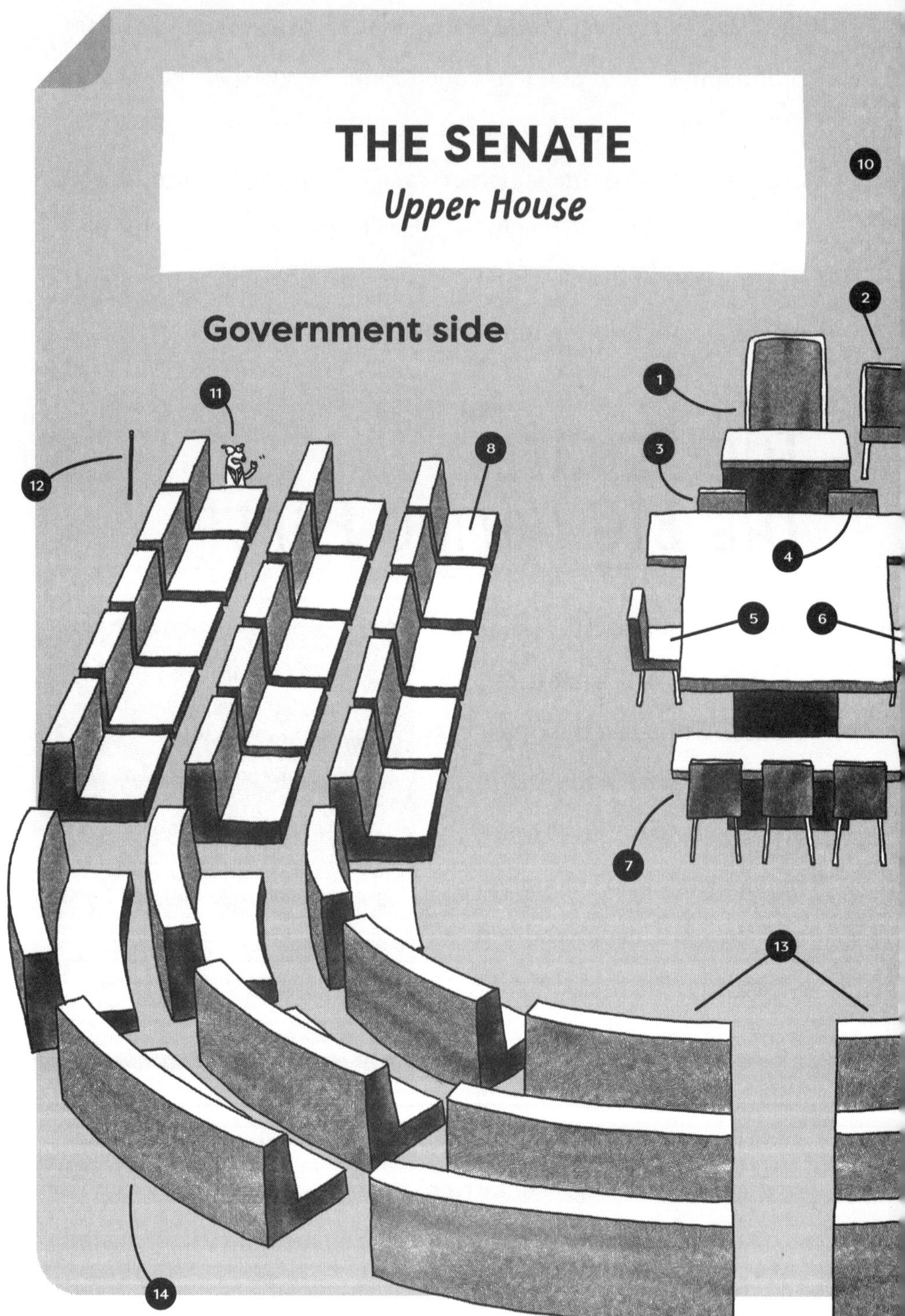
THE SENATE
Upper House
Government side
1
2
3
4
5
6
7
8
10
11
12
13
14

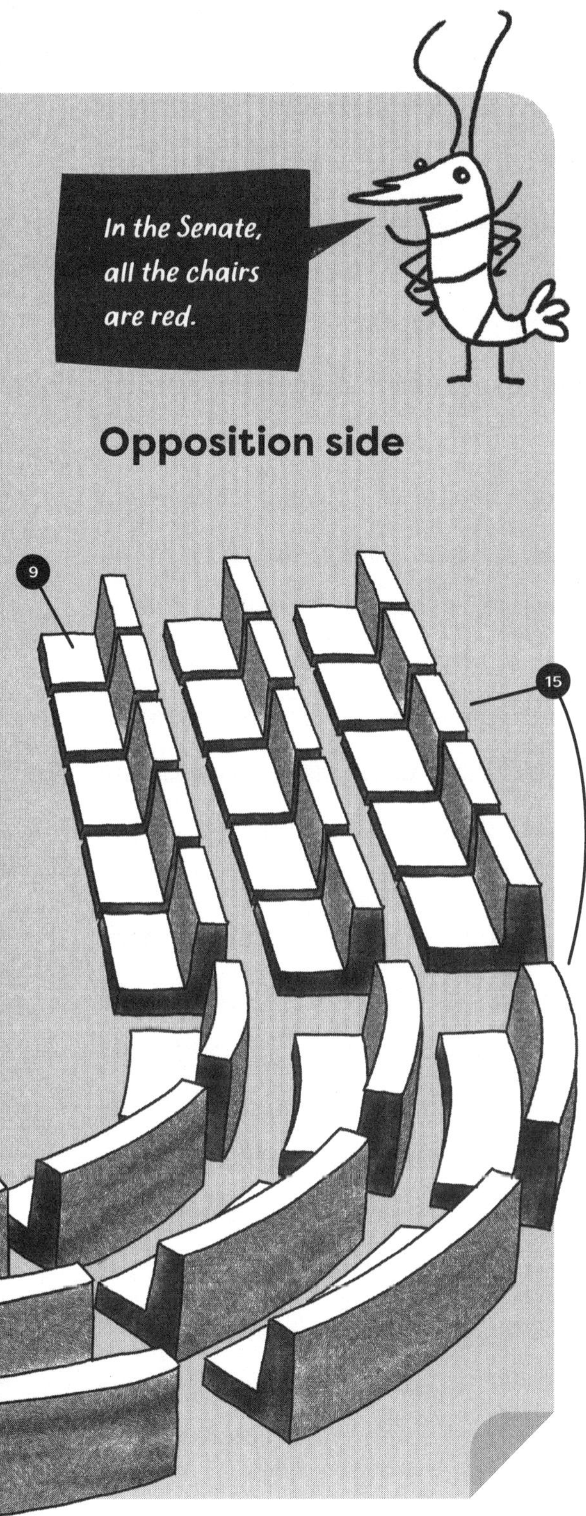

Key

1. President of the Senate
2. Vice-regal Chair (in case the Governor-General needs to sit down)
3. Clerk of the House
4. Assistant clerk
5. Leader of the Government in the Senate
6. Leader of the Opposition in the Senate
7. Hansard person
8. Government ministers
9. Opposition ministers
10. Press Gallery
11. **Usher of the Black Rod***
12. **Black Rod***
13. Crossbench
14. Government backbenchers
15. Opposition backbench

For the House of Representatives, each electorate has its own candidates, so the ballot paper is a short list, usually one person from each party plus any stray Independents. The Senate is a statewide race. All the parties – including the obscure smaller ones – put up whole teams of candidates for each state, and that is why the Senate ballot paper can end up being the size of a bed sheet.

The Senate is often called the states' house, because each state gets 12 senators no matter if it's a big state – like New South Wales – or a teeny-tiny one like Tasmania. If you're a maths nerd, you will be able to work out that this means, in a smaller state, a candidate needs fewer votes to be elected as a Senator. For example, to be elected as a Senator in Tasmania, a candidate only needs about 50,000 votes. But to be elected in New South Wales, it's more like 700,000 votes.

Each state elects 12 Senators, and the territories (the Northern Territory and the Australian Capital Territory) elect 2 each. As you'll remember from the chapter on the Constitution, this system was designed very carefully by the architects of our voting system. To get new laws passed in Australia, **both** chambers have to agree. The Upper House was created to keep watch on the Lower House, and make sure the big states – who get lots of seats in the Lower House – couldn't use their numbers to kick the little states around and make unfair laws like 'Tasmanians have to do all the homework' or 'New South Wales automatically wins the football'.

At each normal election, half of the Senate seats come up for renewal – so, six from each state. Each party will put forward a team of Senate candidates and there are lots of Independents too. It's a more complicated preferential system than the one we talked about earlier, because it's electing multiple candidates.

Up until and including the 2013 election, the system was that the top of the Senate voting paper listed all the party teams and if you wanted to keep it simple you could just put a '1' next to the party you liked. This is called ***'voting above the line'*** and it basically amounted to the voter handing their vote over to that party, and the preferences would be directed according to that party's publicly announced model.

The vast majority of people voted that way, because the alternative was numbering every single box of the individual candidates below the line; peak nerd activity but very satisfying if there was one special individual you particularly wanted to put absolutely last.

This model received a lot of criticism when it turned out an increasing number of very small parties were making deals with each other to direct preferences between them and magically turning quite small numbers of votes into Senate seats.

In 2013, the Senate ballot for Victoria was the largest it had ever been. There were 39 parties and 96 candidates, the paper was more than a metre long, and the font size was so tiny that the Australian Electoral Commission had to distribute magnifying glasses! And one man called Ricky Muir – who ran for the Australian Motoring Enthusiasts Party, which got just 17,122 votes – was astonished to find himself elected to the Senate.

The Coalition Government led by Malcolm Turnbull decided that enough was enough. It legislated changes so that voters could direct their own preferences when voting above the line. Under the new system, when voting above the line you have to number six boxes in order of preference. Or you can vote below the line by numbering at least 12 candidates in order of preference.

It's still a lot more complicated to count than the House of Representatives, and the AEC now uses computers to scan the ballots and calculate the preferences, though humans check that the computers read all the numbers correctly. It can take about a month for the Senate vote count to be concluded.

You might wonder whether the Northern Territory and the ACT ever get a bit sad that they only get two Senators each? The answer is yes, they do. In June 2018, the Labor Member for the Northern Territory-based electorate of Solomon, Luke Gosling, dressed up in a safari suit and sang a song by Meat Loaf to the House of Representatives to draw attention to the fact that the Northern Territory might have been self-governing for 40 years, but it still wasn't a fully-fledged state. His protest didn't do anything, apart from slightly embarrassing his kids.

We'll learn more in future chapters about how a **Bill*** gets passed in Parliament, but the function of a bicameral parliament is that its two chambers have to work together. Usually, the Government introduces laws into the House of Representatives. These are debated and voted on and, unless there is a split in its ranks, the Government will get its way because it has the majority. Then the laws go to the Senate for consideration.

Here's where things get interesting. Because of the way the Senate is elected, it is hardly ever ruled by the Government in the same way the Lower House is. In the Senate, you do find the major parties, but you also get lots of Senators from minor parties such as the Greens, or Pauline Hanson's One Nation.

These Senators are called 'crossbench' senators, not because they are cross, but because they sit in the middle benches of the chamber.

In order to pass its legislation through the Senate to become approved laws, the Government needs to argue and debate and convince the other Senators that the proposed laws are a good idea. As you can imagine, this can get quite complicated.

This is why it often looks like all politicians do is argue. You want to know a secret, though? Of all the proposed laws that come before the Parliament, around 90 per cent are passed with the agreement of all parties. Politicians agree on more than you'd think!

HOW TO DEMOCRACY SAUSAGE

The Short Tale of a Long Snack

Otto von Bismarck, the first Imperial Chancellor of the German Empire, is supposed to have said that laws are, '*like sausages – it's better not to see them being made*'.

I don't agree, as you might have gathered. But it's interesting that Australian voters have become the international pioneers of crossover between democracy and a collection of minced meats stuffed into a casing and grilled at high heat – the democracy sausage!

On Election Day, many polling places will feature a barbecue stall selling sausages in bread, usually to raise money for a local charity. It lends a nice oniony air of celebration to the proceedings! But to observers around the world, it can be controversial. The British Electoral Commissioner, when I interviewed him, said: '*In Britain you'd be arrested for that!*' Now that's an exaggeration, but it's true that in democracies with voluntary voting, there are often rules about offering food or drink to voters as it can be viewed as an 'inducement' or 'bribe' to vote. In Georgia, America, they passed laws making it illegal even to give someone a drink of water in a voting queue!

In the colonial days, Australian elections – like British ones at the time – were rife with candidates bribing voters with 'treats' of pies or mugs of beer.

But when we invented the secret ballot in the 1850s, bribing voters became much harder! And ever since compulsory voting was introduced in 1924, Australia hasn't worried too much about 'inducements' – adults are compelled to vote anyway! So a stall selling tasty morsels near the voting booth is fine.

The term 'democracy sausage' really took off on social media around 2010, when people began sharing maps and tips about where the best sausages were to be found, and which stalls had vegetarian or halal alternatives. And now it's a real thing. Politicians are often obliged to snarfle a democracy sausage on camera as part of their campaign activities, which can lead to some awkward moments, like Labor leader Bill Shorten's bold attempt to eat one sideways in 2016. Look it up! ***Oof.***

MINISTERS AND DEPARTMENTS

Remember walking around Parliament House and the different-coloured carpets? How green is for the House of Representatives side of the building, red is for the Senate, and if you find yourself on blue carpet, ***get out of there fast*** because it means you're in the ministerial wing, where the super-powerful ministers (including the Prime Minister) hang out?

It's time to talk about those ministers and their departments, which are responsible for running all the services that the federal Government provides. And also for collecting the money to pay for those things.

WHAT ARE MINISTERS?

Excellent question. After an election, when the 150 MPs elected to the House of Representatives and the 76 Senators elected to the Senate head to Canberra, the party that has more than half of the seats in the House of Representatives becomes the Government, and the leader of that lucky party becomes the Prime Minister. A number of MPs belonging to that party (usually around 20, but no more than 30) are then selected for special jobs as ministers, which means they will be put in charge of a particular area (often called a **portfolio***). Ministers can come from the House of Representatives or the Senate.

There are many traditional portfolios. The Treasurer is the minister in charge of tax and economic policy. The Health Minister is in charge of doctors and medicines and funding for hospitals. The Transport Minister is responsible for airports, shipping, roads and railways. The Defence Minister is in charge of defence, and... you get the idea. The ministers get their own

Backbenchers are the politicians who did not get picked for special jobs and literally sit behind the ministers in the chambers. Some of them are cool with this, and content themselves with doing their ordinary jobs of representing their electorates. Some of them dream of one day being ministers and do everything they can to get noticed.

offices, and when Parliament is in session they sit along the front bench of both chambers. This is why they are also called **frontbenchers.***

Ministers don't just get nicer offices, more staff and their own chauffeur-driven vehicles; they also each get responsibility for a department in the Australian Public Service. The Public Service covers all sorts of jobs where people are delivering government services, from Tax Office workers to national parks rangers to health officials to spies. They are all arranged into departments, and each department has a Secretary who is the boss of that department. There are *a lot* of jobs. In 2024, the Public Service employed about 185,000 Australians.

The Public Service

Here is a list of the largest Government departments accompanied by my cheat notes as to what they do. If you are doing an assignment on any of these departments, *please* do further research, as I have simplified things brutally! There are more departments, but we don't want to be here all day!

Prime Minister and Cabinet

The head honcho department. Sets policy from the top.

Agriculture, Fisheries and Forestry
Makes rules about farming, fishing, chopping trees down.

Attorney-General's Department
Courts. Judges. *SPIIIIEEEESSSSSS!* (If anyone ever introduces themselves and says vaguely they have a job in the Attorney-General's Department . . . check that person for exploding pens immediately.)

Climate Change, Energy, the Environment and Water
Makes rules about reducing carbon emissions, saving water and *not* chopping trees down. (As one of the departments with very long titles, it's not doing much on the important issue of paper waste, but that's a personal view!)

Defence
Trains Army, Navy and Air Force personnel. Buys planes, boats, submarines and tanks with billion-dollar price tags. (Defence is *expensive*.)

Education

Allocates funding for schools, universities and TAFE.

Employment and Workplace Relations

Can you get a job at age 12? This department will tell you.

Finance

Manages the nation's finances, including salaries for the Public Service and parliamentarians and their staff.

Foreign Affairs and Trade

Argues with other countries about human rights and the importation of widgets.

Health and Aged Care

Funds hospitals, aged care, medicines and – weirdly – sport.

Home Affairs

Immigration, cyber security (more ***SPIES!***) and smuggling (stopping it, not doing it).

Industry, Science and Resources

Research, encouraging inventors and businesses.

Infrastructure, Transport, Regional Development, Communications and the Arts

From roads to ballet! (This is an extremely sprawling department. Geographically and conceptually.)

Social Services

Provides assistance to Australians who are elderly, can't find a job or need support because of a disability.

Treasury
In charge of collecting taxes and advising the Government on the economy.

Veterans Affairs
Looks after people and their families after they leave the armed forces.

Who's Responsible?

The job of the Public Service departments, and the secretaries who run them, is to implement the decisions of the Parliament. And the Minister is responsible to the Parliament for all the triumphs and disasters that take place in their own department. So, if there's a terribly dangerous stretch of road in an MP's electorate, they might ask the Transport Minister about it in Question Time. If there are problems happening in the National Disability Insurance Scheme, the Minister for Social Services will have to explain what's going on. If you've watched Question Time, you will notice that these exchanges do quite quickly become political, and the Minister's response will often incorporate a fair bit of ***'Well, it was much worse when your lot was in Government'***, and so on.

The secretaries of the departments are in charge of carrying out the decisions that the Parliament approves. They manage thousands of workers. They also are regularly hauled in to appear before Senators to be questioned in what are called 'Estimates Committees'. The committee hearings are held to check that public money is being spent responsibly. Many sticky questions are asked. Public servants do not, as a rule, enjoy Estimates Committees, but it's all part of the process of accountability. In the end, it is a convention of our parliamentary system that ministers take official responsibility for everything that happens in their department – even if it isn't their fault.

Ministers also have very serious additional responsibilities under something called the Ministerial Code of Conduct. As ministers, they control the spending of a lot of taxpayers' money. And they are not allowed to misuse it, or spend any of it on themselves, or on things that would help their friends. If they do, that is called a 'conflict of interest', and is a very serious offence. Examples might be if a minister gave a departmental grant to an organisation run by their relative. Or special funding for a school their kid attends.

In 2020, a minister called Bridget McKenzie resigned from the Cabinet because her Agriculture, Fisheries and Forestries Department had given a $36,000 grant to the Wangaratta Clay Target Gun Club. The club had given McKenzie a free membership, so, *ooof!* Conflict of interest. These rules are pretty strict.

The Ministerial Code of Conduct was established by Prime Minister John Howard after he was elected in 1996. It was a very detailed set of rules – so detailed that five of his ministers swiftly had to resign for breaching it. The Code was adjusted after that to make it a bit less tough, but every government since has maintained a version of it.

THE CABINET*

As you know, the Constitution allows the Parliament a maximum of 30 ministers. A third of them are junior ministers, but about 20 of them – the most senior ones – form the Cabinet.

If someone is a 'junior minister', also known as an 'assistant minister', it doesn't mean they're younger than a 'senior minister'. And it doesn't mean they're newer in the job either. Essentially, senior ministers are the more powerful ones who sit in the Cabinet.

The Cabinet meets in a special, super-secure room in Australian Parliament House, just across the corridor from the Prime Minister's Office. Cabinet meetings are always chaired by the Prime Minister, the meetings are top-secret, and, while the Cabinet members may have massive arguments over particular issues, they are all expected to stand by the final decision of the Cabinet once it's made. This is called ***'Cabinet solidarity'***.

Bugs in the Cabinet!

A lot of effort goes into ensuring that the Cabinet Room is as secure as possible. It's on the inside of the building, with no windows to the outside. Its entrance is guarded. And nothing goes in there – chairs, artworks, jugs of water – without being thoroughly checked for electronic listening devices (bugs).

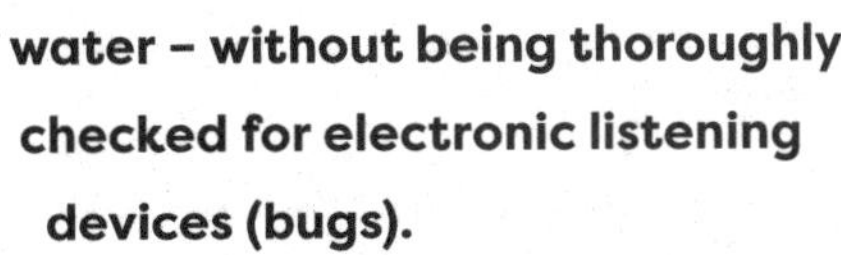

On the ceiling above the large circular Cabinet table is a magnificent carved wooden panel featuring an intricate wreath design of eucalyptus leaves. The artists were given a real talking-to about the need for the work to be secure, and the Adelaide artist who designed the panel – Tony Bishop – decided to add a larrikin touch to the work. If you look closely among the delicate carved leaves, you will find a tiny cicada, a dragonfly and a good old Aussie blowfly hiding. All carved out of native woods by the genius marquetry artist Michael Retter.

On the off-chance you never get to be a Cabinet minister, you can see other examples of Retter's masterful marquetry in a public area of Parliament House. There are 20 of his carved panels depicting Australian flowers, set in a frieze around the walls of the Marble Foyer. Shawn the Prawn gets to gaze at them all day!

Nobody is supposed to say, especially to journalists, what happens in the Cabinet Room. Documents and proposals submitted to the Cabinet, and the records of its discussions, are stamped 'Cabinet in Confidence' and cannot be released publicly for 20 years. These are securely stored at the National Archives of Australia.

Though sometimes, they sneakily do!!

It's a lot of responsibility being a minister, especially a Cabinet minister. And when things go wrong in a minister's department or in the Parliament, things can get very shouty and stressful, and sometimes, ministers will lose their jobs.

Australia's political history has more than 100 instances where a minister has quit or been sacked. Sometimes it's because they've had a big argument with the Prime Minister or can't support a decision that's been taken by the Cabinet. Sometimes they resign because they've breached the Ministerial Code of Conduct. Sometimes they resign because they want to challenge the leadership of the Prime Minister. But sometimes it's for a very specific and strange reason. Please enjoy these ***marvellous*** examples from history.

The Noble Resignation

In 1932, with the Great Depression in full swing and many Australians struggling to feed and clothe their families, the Minister for Markets and Commerce, Charles Hawker, resigned over his government's refusal to reduce parliamentary salaries.

The Awkward Horse Reveal

In early 1940, Trade Minister John Lawson negotiated a special agreement supporting a company called Australian Consolidated Industries to manufacture cars in Australia. It emerged that Mr Lawson was leasing a racehorse from the managing director of the company, a Mr W.J. Smith. Mr Lawson drove all the way to Canberra to resign. He did so even though his Prime Minister, Robert Menzies, said he didn't have to.

The 'I Just Can't Stand You' Resignation

Defence Minister Malcolm Fraser resigned in March 1971 because he had quite simply had enough of his Prime Minister, John Gorton. Describing the PM as 'intolerable', Fraser quit his job in a speech to the Parliament; shortly after, Mr Gorton was deposed and replaced with a new Prime Minister, William (Billy) McMahon. Resigning because you can't stand the Prime Minister was also quite a frequent occurrence during the 2010s, when the prime ministership changed hands multiple times over the course of a decade.

The Old TV Switcheroo Resignation

In 1982, Health Minister Michael MacKellar brought a TV into the country, which on customs forms he described as a black-and-white TV. (Yes, TVs used to be black-and-white.) But it was in fact a colour TV, which attracted a higher customs charge. Mr MacKellar resigned. As did his colleague, Customs Minister John Moore, who initially tried to cover things up.

There's a Bear in There

Another customs-related debacle ensued two years later in 1984 when Special Minister of State, Mick Young, a Labor minister, flew into Australia with his wife only to have border officials search his luggage and find a stuffed Paddington Bear toy. He had not paid customs charges on the bear. Young resigned while an investigation took place, though he was later reinstated. The fate of the bear is unknown.

THE SEPARATION OF POWERS

A central feature of our system of government, and of many democracies, is something called the 'separation of powers'. Basically, that means that no single bit of our system of government gets absolute power.

The checks and balances work like this:

The Parliament makes the laws. But the Australian people vote every three years to elect the Parliament, so if the Parliament is making any particularly bad decisions, the people have the power to change things.

The Executive – the Ministers of the Government, each with their own departments and thousands of employees – work to implement the decisions of the Parliament. The Ministers have to front up in Question Time every day when the Parliament's in session, to make sure they're accountable.

The Public Service, with its departments and employees (also sometimes called the bureaucracy), is permanent. They are supposed to remain outside politics (this principle is called 'impartiality' – it means they have to be neutral). They are not elected positions, and their permanency helps provide continuity and stability to government services. Public servants are held accountable by Senate Estimates Committees.

And finally, you have ***judges***. They are entirely outside the Parliament, but as we know from the Constitution, they have

SEPARATION OF POWERS

THE PARLIAMENT

The King, who is represented by

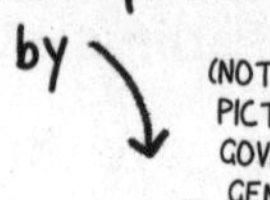

the Governor-General

The Senate

The House of Representatives

THE EXECUTIVE

The King (again), represented by the Governor-General

NO ECHIDNA HAS EVER BEEN GOVERNOR-GENERAL BUT I LIKE THIS DRAWING

The Prime Minister

Ministers

THE JUDICIARY

The High Court of Australia

Federal Courts

the power to block or cancel laws that go beyond the powers of the Parliament.

All in all, the system is supposed to ensure that nobody ever gets so much power that they become a **dictator**.*

If you think this is a confusing system, then pity the United States of America, where the Senate and the Congress and the President all have separate and sometimes conflicting powers! That can get extremely messy.

SHOW ME THE MONEY

Now we have a rough idea of how the Commonwealth Government is organised. But who pays for all this, I hear you ask?

It's a very good question.

Once a year, sometime in May, you might notice politicians out and about arguing loudly about something called the **Federal Budget**. Is it a good Budget? Is it a horror Budget?

Sometimes younger kids get confused and think that there is some big argument going on about a budgie. But you won't ever make that mistake, my friend.

The Federal Budget is published every May, consists of five volumes and is around a thousand pages long.

The Budget is a big list of everything the Government spends money on, and how much each thing costs, for each department. It also lists and counts up all the money the Government collects, and where it collects it from, because every decision the Government makes – and the Public Service implements – either costs or makes money.

Think of the activities of the Government as a giant pie or pikelet.

I am now going to show you:

a) income – or, where the ingredients come from, to make the pie, and

b) spending, or how the pikelet is divided up.

These figures are from the 2025 Budget delivered by Labor Prime Minister Anthony Albanese and his Treasurer, Jim Chalmers. But Budgets change every year. That's why people pay attention to them.

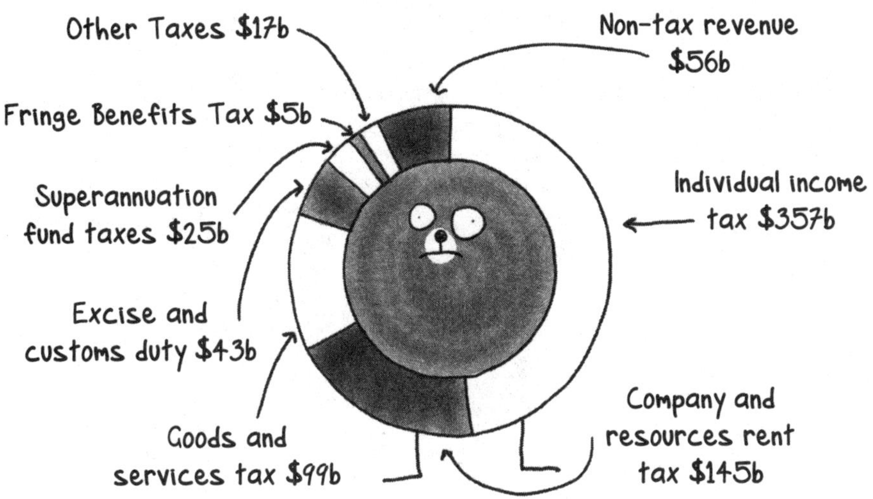

Income, AKA Ingredients for the Pie

Total income = $750.4 billion

- **Income Tax from individuals:** $357.8b
(Comes out of pay packets.)
- **Company Tax:** $145.5b
(Businesses are taxed on their profits.)
- **Goods and Services Tax:** $99.3b
(We pay this at the checkout.)
- **Excise and Customs Tax:** $43.8b
(On things like petrol, alcohol and imported stuff.)
- **Superannuation Tax:** $25.6b
(Taxes on our future savings, whee!)
- **Fringe Benefits Tax:** $5.2b
(Too long to explain here, maybe google it.)
- **Other Taxes (OMG, there are OTHERS?):**
Yes, there are – $17.2b worth!
- **Non-tax Revenue:** $56.0b

GOVERNMENT SPENDING PIKELET

(Money Goes Out)

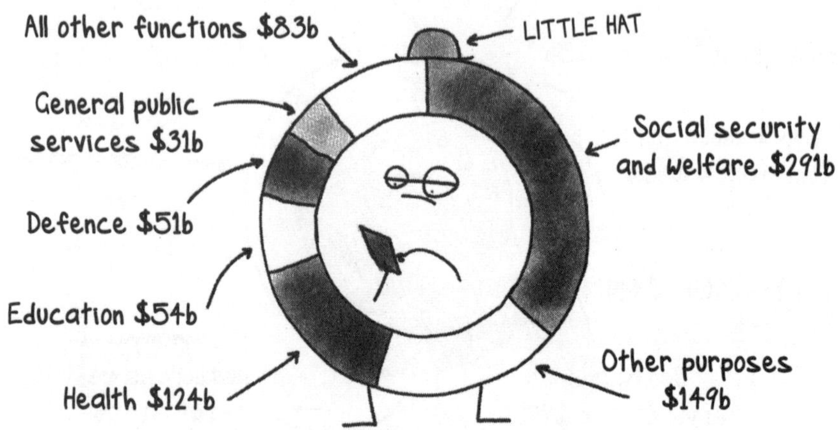

Spending, AKA How We Slice Up the Pikelet

Total spending = $785.7 billion

- **Social Security and Welfare:** $291b
- **Health:** $124.8b
- **Education:** $54b
- **Defence:** $51.5b
- **General Public Services:** $31.4b
- **All Other Functions:** $83.3b
- **Other Purposes:** $149.7b

To be honest with you, I do not know exactly what 'All Other Functions' and 'Other Purposes' are. They are probably a massive pile of smaller bits of spending that don't fit in the chart. You know, stuff like... ***SPIES!***

Now that you are a qualified Budget expert, you will have noticed a few things. Like, the biggest source of Federal Government income is income tax from ordinary Australians. The more you earn, the higher the rate of tax you pay. And the biggest expenditure is on social services and welfare – helping out Australians who can't work or can't afford to support themselves without assistance.

Australia has what is called a progressive tax system, which means that wealthy people pay more, and poorer people pay less, and get more help. We do this to keep things fair.

You may also have noticed that the spending pikelet – at $785.7 billion – is more than the ingredients income – which is $750.4 billion. This means that in this particular year,

The 2025/26 Budget delivered by Labor Treasurer Jim Chalmers in early 2025. Budgets work on 'financial years', which run from 1 July to 30 June, just to be annoying.

the Australian Government spent more than it earned. This is called a **Deficit**,* and we try to avoid that, because we have to top up the pikelet by borrowing money, and then we have to pay interest on that money. It is generally thought better to be in a **Surplus**,* which is when the Government is spending less than it's collecting, but economic and budgetary policy is an endless field of discussion!

Budget Secrecy

Nobody is supposed to know what's in the Budget until it's delivered to the Parliament by the Treasurer, who summarises it in a speech at 7 pm on Budget night, which is usually a Tuesday in May.

The Budget is printed behind locked doors, and is secret (or 'under embargo') until the moment the Treasurer stands in Parliament to make the speech. Journalists are allowed to have a sneak peek at the Budget so they can read it all and understand it before they have to report on it, but they're only allowed to look at it if they agree to be locked up and surrender their phones. They're only allowed out of the 'lock-up' once the Treasurer starts speaking.

Until then, the journalists can't leave the lock-up. They are allowed to go to the toilet, but only if a Treasury official comes with them (not into the cubicle or anything, that would of course be weird).

Why all the secrecy? Because Budgets are full of valuable information and often surprise announcements by the Government. And if the Budget contains measures to, let's say, introduce a sudden new tax on bananas, then if someone knew about it in advance, they could rush out and buy up huge numbers of bananas before the new tax came in and become a banana billionaire overnight. You see what I mean?

Sometimes, details of the Budget 'leak' in advance. This is usually on purpose because the Treasurer wants to get a particularly nice bit – or a particularly terrible bit – out in the open before the general chaos of Budget night.

But there is a famous story involving one of Australia's foremost political reporters, Laurie Oakes, who on one truly magical occasion was leaked the Treasurer's whole Budget speech in advance.

The year was 1980. The Liberal Government of Malcolm Fraser was two days away from handing down the Budget when Oakes got a call.

'*I met a contact in a hotel car park on the Sunday morning. He handed over the Budget speech and gave me 15 minutes to read it,*' Oakes recalls. '*So I gabbled the whole lot into a tape recorder while he went in and had a quick drink, and then I transcribed it back at the office.*'

Laurie Oakes got the scoop! And that is what journalists call 'a very good day at work'.

6 THE PRESS AND PARLIAMENT HOUSE

There are many things that shape the direction of our country. International events can be significant, whether it's the emergence of the COVID-19 pandemic, which caused us to change the way we lived, or Russian President Vladimir Putin's decision to invade Ukraine in 2022, which had a lot of knock-on effects like making energy and power more expensive all around the world, which in turn made *food* more expensive, which made **inflation*** go up, which made interest rates rise, which made it harder to afford a place to live even in Australia even though it is a ***very long way*** from the bits of Ukraine that Vladimir decided he'd like to add to his personal real estate collection.

We live in a connected world. It's full of people who exert power, whether it's with armies or with money or even by leading protest movements made up of ordinary folk... there are ***heaps*** of things that can influence the decisions that governments and politicians make.

The opening of the Provisional Parliament House in 1927 was attended by the Duke and Duchess of York, later to become King George VI and the Queen Mother. It was also attended by King Billy, a Wiradjuri Elder who had walked more than 200 kilometres to attend the opening, even though he was not invited and was not eligible to vote. King Billy, also known as Jimmy Clements, was at first turned away because he was not 'appropriately dressed', but ultimately met with the Duke to discuss Aboriginal sovereignty. King Billy's long march, on which he was accompanied by his friend John Noble – who also went by the name Marvellous – is thought to be the first public protest asserting Aboriginal sovereignty and land rights.

The taking of Aboriginal land by the British colonists without agreement or compensation, and the displacement and suffering of Aboriginal people, is still unfinished business and is the longest-running subject of political protest in Australia.

In fact, the Aboriginal Tent Embassy outside Old Parliament House – now home to the Museum of

Australian Democracy – is believed to be the longest-running continuous protest for Indigenous land rights anywhere in the world.

It began in 1972, when Michael Anderson, Billy Craigie, Tony Coorey and Bertie Williams set up a beach umbrella on the lawns opposite the Parliament in protest against the Government's refusal to recognise land rights for Aboriginal people. The sit-in grew to include tents and campers and placards, and in 2022 celebrated its 50th anniversary.

The freedom to protest or complain about decisions of the Parliament or the Government is a very important part of democracy. Media coverage of protests is a powerful way of spreading the news about injustices and problems that are being overlooked by federal lawmakers.

This particular chapter is about the media.

Now I hate to get all 'when I was your age, phones were plugged into the walls and had a twirly cord and a rotary dial' on you, but the truth is that *they were*. There was no internet. People bought newspapers – actual paper ones – from newsagencies or had them delivered to their front lawns at dawn. Or listened to the radio or watched the 7 pm news bulletin on the telly. That's how people got the news.

Generally by underpaid children!

Now we get news from all sorts of sources. Websites, radio, social media, *Behind the News*, comedians, messages from friends – there are ***so many*** ways to communicate information that it can become very confusing.

And sometimes it's hard to know what's made up and what's real. This is a downside of modern life. There are upsides – like baby capybara photos, and videos of people dancing like their pet parrots, and I am never going to stop being grateful for that – but there's no doubt that the media of today is a lot more shouty and time-consuming and confusing than the media of yesteryear.

What we're going to talk about in this chapter is the way the media has changed over the history of our Parliament, and the effect that's had on how our system of government works. Because it *does* make a difference. Prime ministers and ministers and Opposition leaders and crossbenchers all rely on the media to get their message out. What is the point of a fine speech or a convincing argument if nobody hears it?

The Press Gallery

'The Press Gallery' sounds like a room full of paintings. But actually it's the term to describe the group of reporters who work from inside Parliament House, and whose job it is to tell us all about what's happening in that building. Which laws are being passed, which debates are being had and what's happening in the House of Representatives and the Senate.

Physically, the Press Gallery is a corridor full of slightly messy (okay, ***REALLY*** messy) offices on the second floor of the Senate side of the Parliament building. Lots of different media companies have offices there, from newspapers to TV networks to online news services and radio stations. These reporters also have special seats in the 'gallery' in the chambers of the House of Representatives and the Senate. Reporters can sit and observe the debates and Question Time from on high. But they're not allowed to join in!

The Politician and the Political Journalist

George Reid, who was Prime Minister for a brief but exciting ten months in 1904, is reported to have said to a bunch of newspaper reporters: '*Praise me if you can, blame me if you must, but for Heaven's sake don't leave me alone!*'

And it's true: politicians and political journalists have always had a weird co-dependency thing going on.

On the one hand, politicians and media help each other. Politicians depend on the media to convey their words and ideas to voters. The media depends on politicians for stories, scandal and (more recently) viral videos in which they are secretly filmed picking their noses.

On the other hand, politicians and the media can also hurt each other. Politicians can punish the media by not telling them stuff, or by passing laws that make their job harder. The media can punish politicians by publishing stories about their fancy new beach houses, or blistering critiques of how bad the Prime Minister's housing policy is. Or, you know, the nose-picking thing.

It's fair to say, in general, that the relationship between elected leaders and the media has always been a bit of a ***tense*** one. And the tenseness began well before Australia became a Federation.

Don't Put This in Writing: A Brief History

Five hundred years ago, Britain was ruled by the monarchy (kings only back then) and the Catholic Church. Not many ordinary people could read and write. But the idea of putting written material and information into the hands of ordinary people was already radical.

In the 1500s, there was a chap called William Tyndale who had the brilliant idea of translating the Bible from Latin into English, so that ordinary people might have a better chance of reading and understanding it. This was not a popular decision with the Church. Mr Tyndale's Bibles were burned in great piles at the direction of a very powerful archbishop, and Mr Tyndale himself was executed in 1536.

He was strangled to death and then his body was burned at the stake. A pretty crunchy message there for anyone considering a popular religious publishing venture!

Kings and Parliaments in Britain took turns to make rules that stopped people from printing stuff, especially about them. In 1538, Henry VIII made a law that nothing could be printed and distributed unless it had been approved by the Privy Council, which might sound like a formal body, but really was just a powerful gang of the King's best mates.

What would a perfectly innocent king with a teeny-tiny little hobby of executing his wives have to fear from a free press? I can't imagine, can you?

By the 1700s, the number of newspapers had grown massively, and the press was much freer, but it was ***still*** a criminal offence to publish a direct report of what was said in the parliamentary chambers in Westminster. The other crimes publishers could be jailed for were 'treason' (publishing something that damaged the national interest) and 'seditious libel' (publishing something that brought the Government or its officials into disrespect). All in all, publishers had to be very careful.

Given newspapers and magazines weren't allowed to publish a word-for-word account of what was said in the Parliament, some writers employed extremely sneaky and elaborate devices to get around these laws!

Samuel Johnson – a very great and super-famous British writer, who among many other things was famous for writing the first English language dictionary – was a lowly journalist at this time for a publication called *The Gentlemen's Magazine*. Because they were banned from reporting exactly what was said in the Parliament, the magazine instead published stories that they said were fictional, about a pretend parliament called Lilliput. 'Debates in the Senate of Lilliput' featured politicians with elaborate nicknames, and slightly rearranged versions of the debates that were occurring in the real-life British Parliament. The magazine changed it up enough to avoid arrest, but readers knew who the real characters were and loved the naughtiness of the deceit.

The situation was ridiculous. Why should elected politicians be able to prevent accurate reporting of their words in Parliament? When and how did this change?

Enter a very unusual man called John Wilkes, who in the mid-1700s alternated between being a journalist, being a Member of Parliament and being in jail. Life goals, right there! He was thrown in prison for criticising King George III's speech to the opening of Parliament in 1763 (treason). His supporters staged a rally and a number of them were shot and killed or wounded in what became known as the Massacre of St George's Field. These issues were a big deal at the time.

Wilkes himself was a very odd person. He was jailed again later on separate charges of publishing a very rude poem. He was also a member of an extremely riotous men's club called the Hellfire Club, which was shut down in scenes of chaos after

our man Wilkes procured a mandrill (a large monkey) and dressed it in make-up and human clothes and took it along to the club.

Wilkes's main relevance to this story is that in 1771, after he got out of jail for criticising the King's speech, and he returned to his parliamentary seat, he successfully advocated for the Parliament to drop the ban on reporting its debates. A victory for the free press!

Wild times were ahead in the Golden Age of British newspapers in the 1800s and 1900s. More scandals! More bad behaviour! Possibly, more deeply confused monkeys!

A Hundred Years or so Later, on the Other Side of the Globe

You might recall that the Australian Parliament got itself elected before it actually had its own building. So, from 1901 through to 1927, it borrowed the Victorian Parliament building. Did the Victorian parliamentarians enjoy being kicked out of their building? ***They most certainly did not.*** But they were indeed kicked out, and had to move up the road to the Royal Exhibition Building. Meanwhile, it was in the Parliament House of Victoria, in Spring Street, Melbourne, that the first Australian federal parliamentary Press Gallery was formed.

Space was tight in the building. Prime Minister Edmund Barton – Australia's first PM – lived in an attic upstairs. There were 31 reporters in that first Press Gallery when the Parliament opened in 1901. And they were given space in the building to work, which must have really annoyed the ministers, since only the Prime Minister was given office space and the rest of them had to dash back and forth to offices outside.

Living and working in such close quarters with the Prime Minister and other politicians, the gentlemen of the Press Gallery (for the press were all men at the time) had incredible access to information. And in return, the Prime Minister knew where to find all the journalists. To yell at them if they got something wrong. To give them the cold shoulder and not talk to them, if they were unfair. And in difficult moments, to find and explain to them what his Government was trying to do and ask them to be fair in their reporting.

This close relationship – prime ministers dealing with small bands of newspapermen – persisted for decades.

I'm Sorry, Who's Calling?

When politicians and journalists work in the same building, there are endless mix-ups that can occur. *Herald* journalist Bert Cook, who reported on the early federal Parliament in Melbourne, arrived one day to find a message on his desk. The Prime Minister – Alfred Deakin, then agonising over whether Australia should invest in its own Navy or keep paying the British 200,000 pounds a year to rely on theirs – had left a message asking him to call.

Cook later recalled:

'There was a telephone in the press room which was actually only 20 feet (6 metres) away from the desk in the room across the passage where Deakin sat at his desk. The telephone girl immediately switched me on to Deakin.

"Cook speaking," I said, in a matter-of-fact way. "Understand you want to see me."

"Oh, yes. It's about that Naval agreement. I've been thinking the time is about ripe to give the necessary notice of termination to the British Government."

'I immediately realised that the Prime Minister thought he was talking to his colleague Mr Joseph Cook, the then Minister for Defence.'

Later Sir Joseph, Australia's sixth Prime Minister.

"Excuse me, Mr Deakin," I interrupted. "This is Cook of the *Herald*."

'The dead silence could almost be felt. There was, however, that one little click one can hear when a telephone mouthpiece is quietly replaced.'

THE PRESS GALLERY'S 32ND MAN

From 1901 to 1914, readers of London's *Morning Post* enjoyed a weekly 'Letter' summarising Australian politics. The column was written with great verve and insight by 'A Correspondent' who remained anonymous throughout. Given that the young nation burned through nine prime ministers in its first ten years of existence, there was a lot happening. And the *Morning Post*'s 'Correspondent' was not only incredibly well informed, but pretty free with his opinions.

'*Mr Deakin may well view the position before him with rueful solicitude*,' the Australian Correspondent observed in his *Morning Post* column after Australia's 1903 election, in which Prime Minister Alfred Deakin hung on by the merest margin. '*His own party in his own state, in spite of his appeals, flung away half a dozen seats and imperilled as many more. If his organisation had been half as effective as* (Opposition leader) *Mr Reid's, he could almost have retained his numbers. As it is, the losses of the campaign were all on his side.*'

OUCH. That must have stung a bit for Alfred Deakin to read, right?

Well – the thing is, Deakin *wrote* those words! It was a well-kept secret at the time, but Alfred Deakin – who served as Prime Minister ***three times*** – moonlighted for 13 long years as the

Australian correspondent for the *Morning Post*, a job he took on in 1901 for the quite significant sum of 500 pounds a year. Deakin kept up his secret journalism through all his years as Prime Minister, Opposition leader and minister in the Federation's first decade. He wrote mainly in the mornings, and sometimes enlisted family members to help him post the articles off to London. Over the 13 years, Alfred Deakin wrote more than one million words about Australian politics.

Back then, a lot of politicians took on outside work because being an MP didn't pay very well. But this was a pretty out-there arrangement.

After he'd stopped being Prime Minister, the Morning Post *dropped Deakin's annual pay to 200 pounds a year. Which seems fair.*

PROVISIONAL PARLIAMENT HOUSE

When the first Commonwealth Parliament House opened in Canberra in 1927, it contained accommodation for 48 journalists. The journalists had access to a special balcony in the chambers where they could watch and listen and take notes on what was said. They also received briefings from the Prime Minister and other ministers, and from Government advisers. Different prime ministers had differing degrees of fondness for (or patience with) journalists. Politicians and journalists walked the same corridors. Used the same bathrooms. In fact, the only places politicians could hide from journalists were the Members' Dining Room and the Members' Bar.

This building was meant to be temporary, but ended up hosting the Parliament until 1988. It's now the brilliant Museum of Australian Democracy, which you absolutely should visit!

A pattern that is observable to this very day!

In 1946, a Non-Members' Bar opened, where journalists and parliamentary visitors and staff members and MPs were all welcome. It was a raucous venue, and the scene of many arguments and much loose conversation.

Over time, parliamentarians hired more staff, and the media contingent outgrew its allocation of space. Canberra's Parliament House became very squishy.

OH NO! HERE COMES RADIO

As radio grew in popularity as a way of receiving news, prime ministers like James Scullin (1929–1932) and Joe Lyons (1932–1939) worked out that by speaking on radio, they could get straight into the households of voters without having to do interviews with newspaper journalists.

A big shake-up was on its way. And in 1939, Warren Denning was appointed by the Australian Broadcasting Corporation to become the very first radio reporter in the Press Gallery.

Now, this was controversial. Not so much because the parliamentarians didn't want Denning there – on the contrary, Prime Minister Joe Lyons proposed the arrangement. And not because there was anything wrong with Denning – he was a respected journalist who had worked in the Gallery previously for various newspapers. The problem was that allowing a radio reporter into the Gallery, with its established rhythm of newspaper deadlines, was revolutionary. And upsetting for the newspapermen and their bosses.

Radio deadlines were different from newspaper deadlines. For example, Denning would be able to report an afternoon press conference for that evening's radio news, while the newspaper version of it wouldn't be delivered to the front lawns of their readers until the following morning! The newspaper barons were cross. The reporters were cross. ***A fuss was made.***

The argument was still going in April 1939 when Prime Minister Joe Lyons suddenly died of a heart attack. Rather opportunistically, the newspapermen of the Press Gallery extracted an agreement from the new Prime Minister, Robert Menzies. He would do two press conferences a day: one for the dozens of pressmen, and one for Denning. That way the radio reporter wouldn't be able to copy their homework!

The fact that Menzies agreed to this ridiculous arrangement at all gives you an idea of how powerful the newspapers were. And he kept it up for six weeks. But he quickly got sick of doing two press conferences a day. The newspapers stopped insisting on it once they realised that the arrangement was giving Denning – a very smart journalist – an exclusive half-hour every day with the Prime Minister, which he diligently used to extract some juicy scoops!

You see what I mean – prime ministers and journalists both fear and need each other. The PM doesn't want to annoy the journalists, because the PM wants to be in the newspapers. And the journalists want to keep getting that sweet flow of exclusive information, which they don't want to share with competitors. In politics, information and knowledge carry value and power. That's why that old archbishop burned William Tyndale's English Bibles in the 1500s. That's why Henry VIII banned all publications that weren't personally approved by his posse. And that's why the men of the Australian Press Gallery got all narky when the radio guy tried to join. Information is power, and people naturally want to control the flow of it.

The fuss over the addition of one radio reporter looks comical now, given the incredible transformation that technology has brought to media, and inevitably to the way reporters report on politics and Parliament. That one radio reporter was followed, several decades later, by TV reporters, and then Parliament itself was televised, and then came mobile phones and then came the internet and... well, perhaps it's easier if I do a comparison of the Press Gallery 100 years ago to the Press Gallery of today. You'll see how hugely things have changed.

MEDIA NOW AND THEN

Numbers

The first Press Gallery in 1901 had 31 members (32 if you count the fact that Alfred Deakin was secretly reporting on himself). All of them were men. All of them were newspaper journalists.

Now there are close to 300 working members of the Press Gallery. They work for newspapers, websites, TV and radio networks, and they include photographers and camera operators and researchers and lots of other roles apart from newspaper journalists. More than a third are women.

Access

In the old days, the Press Gallery's small band of newspaper reporters relied on the parliamentary debates, Question Time, briefings from the Prime Minister and whatever gossip they could pick up around the corridors from ministers, backbenchers and parliamentary staff. Canberra was a small town, so journalists could become friendly with politicians, or run into them in the shared bathrooms.

Today, journalists are still free to roam around Parliament House with their special Press Gallery passes, but there are strictly enforced rules about where journalists are allowed to take photos or to film.

Punishment for filming in a prohibited area can be severe – like having Press Gallery passes cancelled or suspended.

Media advisers and press secretaries are now the formal point of contact between journalists and politicians. Back in 1951, only three government figures – Prime Minister Robert Menzies plus two of his ministers – had press secretaries. In 2024, Prime Minister Anthony Albanese had 11 media advisers, and hundreds more worked for ministers and MPs throughout Parliament House.

Sadly, it is no longer common to run into ministers in the bathrooms, as the modern ministerial suites – and all MPs' offices – are equipped with their own loos. But technology has given journalists an incredibly potent new means of access to politicians: the mobile phone. Texting and encrypted messaging apps provide a discreet way for journalists to contact politicians directly, and for politicians to 'leak' information, sometimes even while they are in meetings!

Interviews and Press Conferences

When a major issue is in the news, and the Prime Minister or another minister is being ***pelted*** with questions from news organisations, the MP concerned may choose to do a press conference where they invite journalists to come and hurl questions at them in person. It's a quick way of dealing with them all at once.

In the old days, a press conference involved a nice small group of newspaper reporters with notebooks, who weren't necessarily in a hurry to file their copy. Today, a press conference attracts cameras and sound recordists as well as journalists, and can be beamed live to TV news networks.

In Parliament House, the Prime Minister's press conferences are generally held outside the back door of the Prime Minister's Office, in the Prime Minister's Courtyard. In winter, this makes for very chilly feet.

One day I'm going to go through the records of prime ministerial press conferences in winter compared to those in summer and see if my suspicion is correct that the winter ones wrap up faster. An interesting question for accountability!

Politicians also do question-and-answer sessions when they're on the road, in other cities, or on the campaign trail.

These are less formal and called 'doorstops'. If you see a doorstop in the wild they can look pretty strange – one politician standing in a park or on a street corner, surrounded by a shoving, yelling mob of journalists, camera operators and sound technicians with long fluffy boom mikes.

If a politician knows they have to answer questions on an issue but doesn't like the idea of being asked very HARD questions, they might call a press conference at very short notice in a city that's not Canberra. That way, the Canberra political journalists won't be able to make it there in time.

Deadlines

By the 1930s, the gentlemen of the press wrote their stories on typewriters and sent them to their news desks by means of telex machines. Or they read the copy out loud over the phone to a waiting typist in their distant newsroom. They had one deadline a day! Plenty of time to interview lots of people, check facts and make absolutely sure they had everything right. The correspondent for Sydney's *Herald* back then had a very different life from that of a correspondent for the same newspaper now.

Today, those newspapers have migrated online to websites where the challenge is to break news as quickly as possible and provide updates as soon as they come to hand. Reporters typically file multiple stories a day. They might also make videos or podcasts, do radio interviews and post on social media. All while attending press conferences, conducting interviews, reading reports and press releases, chasing people for interviews and checking facts. On busy parliamentary days, it gets extremely ***hectic***.

It's hectic for MPs as well. In the old days, they used to deal with questions and demands from a small number of journalists, most of whom they knew personally. But a busy politician's media routine is now exponentially more demanding. They juggle live interviews and debates on 24-hour news channels like ABC News and Sky News while fielding questions from reporters around the country, while also running their own websites, newsletters and social media...the list is endless. Plus, they also have to do their main job of debating legislation, making sure they don't miss votes, meeting with constituents and so on. There is absolutely no doubt that the explosion in media over the last few decades has hugely changed and complicated the working lives of both politicians and the journalists who report on them.

Restrictions on the Media

The lives of journalists have improved since the 1700s in Britain when they could be jailed for reporting on parliamentary debates, but our nation has used and continues to use other methods of controlling what gets published. Here are some of the ways that governments and the Parliament have controlled or limited what media organisations can report or publish.

National Security Rules

When Australia officially joined World War One in 1914, the Parliament hastily passed the *War Precautions Act*, which gave the Government power to censor what newspapers were allowed to publish about the war. For instance, when the disastrous invasion of Gallipoli occurred, the first official accounts published in Australia hailed it as a triumph to keep citizens' spirits up. This is not unusual. Many countries throughout history have censored the press in times of war. It's intended to limit the possibility of valuable information falling into the hands of the enemy. Or to keep spy operations secret. Or to keep public morale high by not telling citizens just how badly the war is going.

In 1952, the Australian Government adopted a British Government invention called the 'D Notice'. The 'D' stands for 'Defence', and D Notices were voluntary arrangements negotiated between the Defence Department and media organisations who agreed not to report on certain things, on the basis of national security. The group hasn't met since 1982, but there are a handful of D Notices still in effect. One of them is about reporting on ASIO (Australian Security Intelligence Organisation), our spy agency. Another one of the D Notices is about reporting on the location of the Petrovs, a Russian couple who defected from the Russian Embassy in 1954. Mr Petrov was a **KGB*** spy, and his defection kicked off a major scandal in Australia that was reported around the world. It's actually funny that the Australian media is still technically barred from publishing stories about the whereabouts of the Petrovs. They've both been dead for decades!

The last time D Notices were seriously discussed was in 1995, when the *Sydney Morning Herald* and the ABC landed a ***hot scoop*** – that Australian spies for ASIO had successfully planted bugs in the Chinese Embassy in Canberra while it was under construction. The story was true, but the Australian Government did not want ASIO's sneaky behaviour to be exposed. Foreign Minister Gareth Evans took out an order in the Federal Court preventing journalists from printing or broadcasting the story and, dramatically, the ABC's report was pulled from the TV news programme shortly before it was due to be broadcast.

In the end, the stories were published. Even in 1995, the media was big enough and varied enough that keeping a lid on such a juicy story was tricky. Today, such censorship is very hard to achieve and as a result is rarely attempted.

Privilege

There is a law of the Parliament that has a particular relevance to media and journalists, called the *Privileges Act*. This Act is about the 'privileges' that apply to MPs. One of them is ***'parliamentary privilege'***, which means that an MP can stand up in the House of Representatives or the Senate and say anything they like without fear of reprisal or penalty. This is an *incredibly* significant superpower, and when new MPs arrive in Parliament, they are advised they should use it very sparingly.

Australia's Privileges Act *was passed in 1987, formalising our rules, but the concept of parliamentary privilege was inherited from British Parliament and is mentioned in the Constitution.*

One of the main restrictions on freedom of speech in Australia is our **defamation*** law. If you go on TV or radio or social media or any other platform and loudly announce 'The Prime Minister is a corrupt criminal and also he is only pretending to like Taylor Swift', then there is a strong possibility you have just defamed the Prime Minister. And possibly Taylor Swift. You could get sued, in which case you would have to go to court and prove the truth of your remarks or cop a hefty fine.

But if you were a Senator, and you said these words in the chamber, you would be immune from prosecution because of the *Privileges Act*.

Do politicians ever take advantage of parliamentary privilege to stand up and say defamatory things about their enemies? Yeah, that has happened. But not that often. Taking advantage of parliamentary privilege is viewed as an extreme thing to do, and it's generally frowned upon. Parliamentary privilege also extends to the evidence heard by parliamentary committees, so that witnesses can give honest evidence without worrying about getting sued.

Parliamentary privilege also protects committee reports from publication until the report has been officially 'tabled' in Parliament.

The *Privileges Act* makes it an offence to intimidate an MP or to prevent them from doing their job independently and well. And it's this last element of parliamentary privilege that led – in 1955 – to the one instance in Australian history of the Australian Parliament directly voting to throw a journalist in jail.

Newspaper Jailbirds!

On 28 April 1955, the *Bankstown Observer* published a story about the area's MP, the Labor Member for Reid, a man called Charles Morgan. The article claimed that Morgan – a former lawyer – had been involved in a corrupt immigration scam before he entered Parliament. Mr Morgan – who hotly denied the allegations –

complained to the Parliament's Privileges Committee, claiming he was being intimidated and bullied by the *Bankstown Observer*, which was trying to restrict his work as an MP by printing lies about him in his own electorate.

The Privileges Committee met over several days in secret and concluded that – yes – a breach of privilege had indeed occurred. The owner of the *Bankstown Observer*, Mr Raymond Fitzpatrick, and his editor, Mr Frank Browne, were called to appear 'at the bar' of the House of Representatives to explain themselves.

'Appearing at the bar' of the Parliament is an ancient and rare tradition. Right up the back of the House of Representatives chamber, where the door leads out to the Members' Hall in the direction of the Senate, there is a brass bar that slots in sort of across the doorway. This is where ordinary people can be brought in to be questioned.

Fitzpatrick and Browne had to stand behind the bar while the Parliament voted on a motion from Prime Minister Robert Menzies that they should be jailed for 90 days for their contempt of the Parliament. The chamber voted in favour of the motion, and Fitzpatrick and Browne were hauled away to Goulburn Prison. They were the first and – so far – last Australians to be jailed by a vote of the Parliament.

This story tells us a few things. How extensive the powers of the Parliament can be, for one thing. Jailing two men who've never had a day in court? ***That's pretty extraordinary.***

Extraordinary, too, that a Liberal-dominated chamber would take such extreme action to defend the honour of a Labor MP. Was it a sign of noble principles that political enemies would drop their weapons in order to defend an opponent against the indignity of journalistic intimidation?

Guess again.

Mr Fitzpatrick, apart from being a newspaper proprietor and local businessman, was also a very committed Labor enemy of Mr Morgan's. Mr Morgan had – under the protection of parliamentary privilege – described Fitzpatrick as a war profiteer and a corrupt businessman. Fitzpatrick hired Browne – later described as '*a hard-bitten, hard-drinking journalist of far right-wing persuasion*' and a '*ratbag of the highest order*' – expressly to write stories trashing Morgan.

Browne was best known for his gossip column, 'Things I Hear', which regularly defamed politicians of all sides. And three months before the story about Morgan, Browne had published an item about Prime Minister Robert Menzies, describing his failure to enlist for military service when Australia joined World War One, and labelling him a coward.

Aha! So *that's* why the PM was so annoyed!

Politics and journalism are full of people who are there for good reasons, but like all systems and democracies, sometimes it is not straightforward. Media proprietors who use their power to inflict damage on personal enemies. Politicians who use their parliamentary privilege to settle the score. Journalists (very rare ones!) who publish misinformation because they think they can get away with it. Overreaches of parliamentary power that are still wrong even though they've been used to punish scoundrels. It's complicated!

The Future Is ... Let's Face It. Whatever is Printed Here is Already Out of Date!

Changes in the media are happening ***extremely fast*** and the Press Gallery is less central to the way we hear about politics than it was 100 years ago, when people mainly got their news from newspapers.

Today, only about 4 per cent of people get their news from newspapers. TV is the main source of news for 36 per cent of Australians, 28 per cent get their news online, 25 per cent from social media and 6 per cent from radio. That's why during the 2024 election campaign the Prime Minister, Anthony Albanese, and the Opposition leader, Peter Dutton, spent lots of time going on podcasts and talking to social media influencers, as well as doing interviews and press conferences. They need the media! Politicians can't really succeed anywhere unless they can get their message out!

MAKING LAWS

If you are lucky enough to visit Parliament House while the Parliament is sitting, chances are you'll go to see Question Time. Why? Because Question Time in the House of Representatives is the liveliest part of the parliamentary day, and you're certain to see the Prime Minister, the Opposition leader and the vast majority of the other MPs in the chamber.

Held at 2 pm on sitting days, Question Time is 90 minutes' worth of Opposition and crossbench MPs firing questions at Government ministers, and ministers defending themselves and the work of their Government, while everybody shouts and heckles. It can get ***very messy***, and loud, and sometimes the Speaker has to throw politicians out of the chamber.

Though perhaps some are possibly a teeny bit inspired!

Visiting school groups are often absolutely horrified by the unruly behaviour witnessed at Question Time. And visiting politicians from the United States of America – where they don't have Question Time, and the convention in their Congress is not to interrupt another member while they are on their feet speaking – often look quite green around the gills after witnessing this particularly Australian spectacle.

*Senators have their own Question Time in the Senate, though it's less of a public drawcard. (I'm sorry, Senators, you are a **VERY** important part of the parliamentary process, but that's just the harsh truth.)*

In the Senate chamber, each seat has a little earpiece where you can listen in to the other chamber. Sometimes you can see them listening in to the other Question Time!

But Question Time isn't the most important thing that the Parliament does. It's just the most famous part. There's a difference. And MPs aren't usually all in the chamber at the same time, shouting at each other, as they seem to be during Question Time. ***The most important job the Parliament does is to make new laws.*** This chapter is all about how that happens.

Laying Down the Law

New laws affect all of us. They change our lives by changing the rules that apply to us as citizens. New laws might alter the amount of tax we pay, or change the rules that govern workplaces.

Like the Right to Disconnect laws that were passed in 2024, making it illegal for a boss to demand their employees be available to respond to text messages 24 hours a day.

Or they might change the way schools are funded. Or – as was first announced by the Albanese Government in 2024 – ban under-16s from using social media.

Perhaps you have heard about that one?

Because making new laws is such a big deal, there's a very strict process around how it is done. Rules are in place to ensure that every elected Member of Parliament gets an input into every new law, and as many experts as possible are consulted. It doesn't just happen overnight! Except in special circumstances of urgency, when laws can be passed very quickly.

The Strawberry Sabotage Scandal

One of the quickest-ever laws made in Australian history was 2018's *Criminal Code Amendment (Food Contamination) Act*. Street name: the Strawberries Law.

In August of 2018, reports emerged from Queensland and Western Australia that shoppers had found sewing needles inside strawberries they'd bought. ***Yes, I agree: weird.*** Who would put a needle in a strawberry? As word spread across media, people started to panic. What if they accidentally ate a needle? Who was doing this? Where would the next strike be? Was pavlova now a high-risk food?

More needles were discovered in punnets of strawberries. People exchanged jam recipes and urged each other to puree strawberries and sieve them to reduce the risk of injury. Strawberry sales plummeted. Strawberry farmers despaired. The mood was hectic. And, seeing as Australians on average eat more than ***two kilograms*** of strawberries a year *each*, the Strawberry Sabotage Scandal quickly became a national crisis.

When the first needle was found in the first strawberry, Scott Morrison had been the Prime Minister of Australia for approximately one week.

This was during an unfortunate phase in Australian politics where we burned through one prime minister about every two years.

Mr Morrison, as a bright shiny new Prime Minister, was very keen to be seen to ***do something*** about the crisis. '*Any idiot who thinks they can go out into a shopping centre and start sticking pins in fruit and thinks this is some sort of lark or put something on Facebook which is a hoax, that sort of behaviour is reckless*,' he told Parliament.

Berry keen, you could say.

Mr Morrison's office swiftly drafted new laws imposing a penalty of up to 15 years in prison for anyone found deliberately contaminating food, and the Prime Minister called upon Parliament to pass the new laws right away. '*I expect nobody goes home until that's done*,' he declared. And sure enough, the Strawberries Law was passed the very same day.

One woman was eventually arrested and charged with putting needles in strawberries, but the charges were later dropped. I can find no trace of anyone ever actually being put in prison under the Strawberries Law.

JAIL!

This raises an important point about politicians and laws. Sometimes laws are planned in advance and designed over a long period to do certain things. But on other occasions, laws are passed very quickly to respond to a perceived national crisis. The main purpose is to make it very clear, during a time of fear or uncertainty, that politicians are ***doing something***.

A new law – once the whole process is complete – is called an **Act of Parliament**,* and it's only at the very end of that process that the new law actually takes effect.

Before that, when it's just a proposal, working its way through the Parliament, it's called a Bill. It's not a proper law, or Act, until it has gone through the following steps (deep breath):

Possibly considered by committees, sometimes more than one
MY FIRST BILL
Sometimes amended
?
MY FIRST BILL
Sometimes bounced back and forth between the two chambers
REPS
SENATE
BOING
BA-DOING
Folded into the shape of an orchid
Read a third time
THE AYES HAVE IT!
Voted on finally by both Houses
Sent to the Governor-General
MY FIRST LAW
And signed into law
Exhausting, right?

Where Do Bills Come From?

Bills can originate in the House of Representatives or the Senate (unless they are Bills about the spending of money, in which case they have to be introduced in the House of Representatives). Theoretically, Bills can be introduced by Government ministers, by junior ministers (known as backbenchers), by Government MPs, by Opposition MPs or by crossbenchers.

This makes it sound like anyone can bung a Bill into the system and have a fighting chance of making it into law! But realistically, the Government has the most votes in the House of Representatives. So it's mainly the Government's Bills that get debated and progressed through the system.

If you go to the Parliament of Australia's website and click on 'Bills before Parliament', you'll find a handy-dandy list of all the Bills that have been introduced to the Parliament and are currently awaiting attention.

Some of them move through the process and duly become Acts. But lots of Bills proposed by the Opposition and crossbench MPs sit there getting mouldy. Mind you, sometimes they are called things like 'A Bill to Expose the Horrible Beastliness of the Government's Failure to do Anything About Vertical Fiscal Imbalance'. When they have titles like that, you know most likely they aren't going to work their way through Parliament.

If you crack open the text of any listed Bill and read it, you'll notice that they are written in a very technical, lawyer-y way. It might make your eyes sting a bit to read, but it's important Bills are written in the same style to make sure that they are clearly expressed, consistent with each other, and cover every legal base.

Parliament has a very helpful group of people who work in the Office of Parliamentary Counsel who are experts in writing Bills. They help MPs and Senators draft the Bills they want to introduce.

I'll give you an example. My children would love me to be banned from using teenage slang because it's so incredibly ***cringey*** and I always get it wrong. They would also absolutely love to be able to give this ban the force of law.

If they were to have a stab at writing a Bill to this effect, it might say something like: 'Annabel Crabb is banned from using the words ***"slay"***, ***"sigma"*** and ***"triggered"*** at all times. Penalty: 20 years imprisonment.' Makes sense, doesn't it?

But the wonderful world of legislation doesn't work like that. Because any law passed has to survive the scrutiny of courts and lawyers and so forth, Bills drafted for Parliament are written in a particular legal style, careful to mention the explicit Commonwealth power that is being exercised in the Bill.

As you know from the Constitution chapter, there are strict divisions between what is a Commonwealth responsibility and what is a state responsibility.

When you're writing a Bill for the federal Parliament, you have to make it very clear which area the proposed law is relevant to, which power it uses, that it's within the powers of the Commonwealth and what its exact effects are going to be.

Assuming they could convince a Member of Parliament to even consider introducing it, let's have a look at how my kids' proposed ban might fare. Would it even be within Commonwealth powers to legislate such a ban?

Here's where my kids get lucky. I work at the Australian Broadcasting Corporation, which is a Commonwealth-funded public broadcaster. A quick check of the Australian Constitution (Section 51) reveals that broadcasting and telecommunications are part of the responsibilities of the federal Government. ***Bingo!*** My kids could totally argue that it's technically within the powers of Parliament to ban an ABC employee from using certain words.

But first the Bill itself would need to be written in a form more precise than the version I suggested earlier.

For starters, it would be called something like 'The Australian Broadcasting Corporation Amendment (Eliminating Maternal Embarrassment) Bill 2025'. And it would set out in very careful legal language the exact terms I would be banned from using, where I would be banned from using them, whether I would be allowed to use any of those words in another context and so on. Every possible interpretation would need to be covered, and every possible unintended consequence considered. Why? Because when the Parliament passes sloppily worded legislation, the laws are vulnerable to being challenged through the court system.

And let me tell you right now, kids, Mum's definitely gonna get her lawyers onto this one. And when I go to court, I WILL EAT AND LEAVE NO CRUMBS.

The vast majority of Government Bills are drafted and presented by the minister responsible for the department in question, with assistance from their staff.

Often, ministers try to introduce new laws following through on promises made during an election campaign. Election campaigns are like sales pitches where each major party makes a pile of promises about what they'll do if they win the election. Maybe they'll promise to cut taxes, or to pay for new public housing, or to increase financial assistance to university students. Whichever party wins the election then will generally draft Bills that bring about the changes they've promised.

Sometimes governments will go to an election worried that they might lose, and make a lot of big and impressive campaign promises. If they then somehow win, they kind of have to do the things they promised, and that can get extremely awkward.

Sometimes governments will draft new Bills that weren't mentioned during the election campaign. In some less-common instances, these are because they are unpopular ideas that the Government didn't much want to mention. Usually, they are drafted to respond to an unforeseen complication or development that's happened since the election. Like the Strawberry Crisis of 2018. Or the arrival of the COVID-19 pandemic in 2020, which required a whole bunch of new laws at the federal and state level.

But whatever the reason, and no matter who's proposing a Bill, every Bill has to follow a similar process before it becomes an Act.

Step One: Bill Gets Thought Of

If it's a Government Bill, the first step is that the Government has to decide that it definitely wants to create a new law. Usually, this involves the minister concerned taking the proposal to a meeting of Cabinet and getting everybody's (especially the Prime Minister's) agreement that it needs to be done.

This sounds like it should be simple, but sometimes it isn't. Most new laws cost money. They might involve a whole new area of expenditure or create a whole new area of work that needs to be done by someone.

Even the very simple-sounding proposal that Annabel Crabb be banned from using the word 'Slay" will cost money. There's the cost of employing people to follow me around 24 hours a day keeping tabs on what I say. In the event that I break the new law, then I will need to be arrested and placed in custody, which isn't free. Then a trial will need to be held to establish my guilt or innocence, which costs a fortune. If I'm found guilty and I get the maximum penalty, then I'm going to need to be kept in prison for 20 years, and prisons are EXPENSIVE.

Running a government involves thousands of decisions (some of them very tough) about which issues should be addressed and which might have to be ignored.

Arguments over Bills are made very energetically in Cabinet. Picture the sort of discussion that the proposed Eliminating Maternal Embarrassment Bill 2025 might provoke:

In the Case *For* the Bill

Minister for Youth Affairs

I urge you, Prime Minister, to support this important legislation. The youth of Australia have suffered enough. We've banned them from social media. They'll never be able to afford to buy a house. They got locked down in the pandemic and had to do classes by Zoom. Some of them are forced to play SPORT. Surely – ***SURELY*** – we need to be able to guarantee them an Australia in which they are not obliged to witness a 50-something woman trying to be cool and failing? Prime Minister, may I remind you that these young people will be able to vote some day? Let's not make them hate us, because they'll be 18 sooner than you think.

In the Case *Against* the Bill

Minister for Communications

Prime Minister, I must urge you to ignore the foolish proposal advanced by my colleague. It's easy for the Minister for Youth Affairs to make herself popular with young people by suggesting this new law. But it's my department that will need to find the money to monitor Annabel Crabb and her language. I don't know if you've noticed, but that lady is ***CHATTY***. Policing her is going to be expensive. How is this a good use of federal funds? To say nothing of the precedent it would set? Today, it's banning an ABC employee from saying 'slay'. What's next? Banning Bluey from saying 'woof'? Honestly, the ramifications here are endless and I just think the whole idea should be vigorously resisted.

When Cabinet is divided on how to proceed on a particular idea, it's usually the Prime Minister who makes the final call. And if they decide to back the Eliminating Maternal Embarrassment Bill 2025, the next step is for it to be shown to all the other Government MPs and Senators before it's formally introduced to the Parliament as a Bill.

Sometimes (and this is rare) Government MPs and Senators object at this point, and an argument ensues. This can pan out differently depending on which party is in government. The Labor Party's meeting of all its MPs and Senators is called the **Caucus**.* It's what's called a ***'binding'*** group, which means that all members are obliged to vote in favour of Government legislation. The Liberal Party works differently. Its members are allowed to vote against their own Government, which is called 'crossing the floor'. Crossing the floor as a Labor MP can get you expelled from the Labor Party. Doing it in the Liberal Party just makes you unpopular. And in practice, it doesn't happen very often. Crossbenchers – because they don't belong to a major party – can vote whichever way they like, on any Bill.

Once the Cabinet has decided to introduce a certain piece of legislation, the most common outcome is that the Caucus or **party room*** will approve it. The minister responsible then advises the Clerk of the House that a Bill is on the way, and the Clerk pops the Bill on the Notice Paper for the next day of sitting.

The Notice Paper is an incredibly important part of the average sitting day in Parliament. It's like a very detailed diary, and it tells the MPs what's happening that day. Things like what Bills are to be introduced, Bills to be debated, and all other fixtures of the parliamentary day like Question Time and 'Matters of Public Importance', a daily slot where MPs get to harp on about any subject that is particularly vexing them. The Notice Paper is maintained by the Clerk, who is like the responsible adult of the chamber. The Clerk is not elected but is an employee of the Parliament.

Step Two: First Reading

The first outing a proposed Bill has in the Parliament is called the ***'First Reading'***.

The First Reading is when the person proposing the Bill (usually a minister) stands in the chamber and announces the name of the Bill and hands a signed copy of the whole thing to the Clerk. This doesn't mean the entire text of the Bill actually gets read out – some of these things are *long*, and the legalistic language used would probably put everyone to sleep – but copies are distributed to all the MPs. Usually at this point the minister moves that 'This Bill will now be read a second time'.

Step Three: Second Reading

The Second Reading – once again – does not mean the entire Bill is read out loud. The Second Reading is actually the opportunity for ***speechifying***, not reading. It begins with a stirring speech from the minister or MP moving the Bill, explaining in detail why the Bill has been proposed, what it is intended to do and why it would be absolutely disastrous on every level for this Bill not to become law as swiftly as possible. This is commonly an opportunity for ministers to make extravagant mention of the people who will be better off under the new laws, and perhaps a little less mention of any people who might be worse off. The minister might additionally take the opportunity to point out that it is really only *their* party with the decency, courage, handsomeness and vision to move (present) this Bill, and perhaps summarise the historic failings of their political opponents in this particular area.

Honestly, I agree, these steps could be a bit more accurately named.

The parliamentary chambers are always places of political argument, and it is rare for a politician to pass up the opportunity to compare themself favourably to the jokers on the other side of the chamber!

This initial speech is really important, because future historians (and judges, if things wind up in court) will go back to the official transcript, the Hansard, and read the speech carefully to understand exactly what the Government's intentions were when its minister proposed this law.

After the minister (or proposer) has finished speaking, the debate is ***'adjourned'***, which is a fancy procedural word meaning 'Let's pick this up later, folks'. The adjournment gives all the other MPs a chance to read the Bill, to think about whether they agree with it, to go around and ask experts and colleagues what they think, and to consider whether they want to try 'amending' the Bill, which is a fancy procedural word meaning to chop bits out or add bits on.

Sometimes there will be a long break between the minister's second reading speech and the resumption of debate. Here are some reasons such a delay might happen at this point:

1) There are a lot of Bills knocking around and the Government decides there are others it'd rather get done first.

2) The Parliament goes on a break.

3) The Government realises, after it's introduced the Bill and the minister's delivered the second reading speech

and everybody's had a good look at what's being proposed, that the Bill is going to be a bit harder to pass than first thought. Its members might learn this in a number of ways. Maybe they'll see media interviews with key crossbenchers, or the **Shadow Minister,*** or an important industry group or community organisation, raising issues or objections the Government wasn't expecting. Maybe they'll notice that an angry mob has formed outside the Parliament shrieking in protest! All of these things can provide strong reasons for a Government to hit the go-slow on a Bill or review its approach.

4) The Government goes off the whole idea for its own mysterious reasons. During the tumultuous years between 2007 and 2018, when we changed prime ministers about every ten minutes, many a Bill got abandoned halfway through the process because the PM whose idea it was suddenly became an ex-PM. Politics can be a messy business!

In some cases, a Bill won't proceed at all after the Minister's second reading speech. It'll just sit there on the 'Current Bills' list being ignored with all the other unloved ones or be withdrawn entirely. But more usually, a Government Bill will be brought back for a second reading debate, which is where the other MPs get a chance to give speeches declaring their views on the Bill. Supporters will explain why they support it. Opponents will explain why they think it's the worst idea they've ever heard.

And when everybody who wants to speak has done so, the Speaker will invite the House to vote on the minister's motion that ***'this Bill will now be read a second time'***.

STEP FOUR: CONSIDERATION IN DETAIL

This is the step where the debate turns to the nitty-gritty of the proposed legislation and where it's open to MPs to call into question each and every clause and dot point. MPs are allowed to move their amendments, which are proposals to change this word, or sentence, or take it out altogether, or change the penalty from 20 years to 12 years, or whatever.

'Consideration in Detail' can happen in both chambers. If the House is chock-full of Bills, debate can also happen in the Federation Chamber, which is a large committee room designed to be a secondary chamber for the Lower House. It's less fancy-looking than their main chamber, but MPs' speeches there are recorded by Hansard in exactly the same way and have the same status as speeches in the main chamber. Basically, the Federation Chamber is there so that MPs can drone on to their hearts' content while allowing the main chamber to get along with other business. Voting on decisive clauses and motions, though, only happens in the main chamber.

This process of amendments and discussion clause by clause, mind you, will only happen if there is objection or opposition to the Bill. And by this stage, both the Government and the Opposition will have a pretty good idea of who supports the Bill and who doesn't. If everyone is in favour – and as mentioned earlier, the amazing truth of our argumentative Parliament is that about 95 per cent of Government Bills actually do get passed in the end – then the Bill will be voted through without amendments or clause-by-clause debate. In which case it will pass to the Third Reading stage.

STEP FIVE: THIRD READING

You will be stunned to learn that the Third Reading stage *also* does *not* involve reading the whole Bill out loud. This stage is quick and is a formality – either because no objections or amendments have been proposed, or because they've already been made and voted on. The Third Reading stage is a simple vote of the chamber, and if the Bill is approved then it will continue on its merry way to the Senate.

Step Six: The Red Room of Pain

After the Clerk of the House writes a certificate confirming that the Bill has passed the Lower House, the Speaker of the House writes a short message to the President of the Senate, asking if the Senate would please take a look at this Bill. The Bill is printed out, the certificate and message are attached, and the whole bundle is walked over to the Senate Chamber by the **Serjeant-at-Arms.***

This walk's only about 100 metres, and of course the Bill and its attachments could very easily be emailed across, but the tradition of the Serjeant-at-Arms carrying it over is ancient. And keeping track of these 'conversations' between the two chambers is actually quite important, especially if you get to the point where the two chambers disagree with each other. Of which more in a moment.

Now that the Bill has arrived in the Senate, it's the Senators' turn to go through the same steps – first reading, second reading and third reading.

Of course you know by now that none of these stages means the whole Bill is literally being read out.

This is where the fun begins. Because while the Government usually has the most votes in the House of Representatives, this is not usually the case in the Senate.

What does this mean in practice?

Well, it means the Government has two choices. Either it can convince the Opposition to come around to its way of thinking (sometimes the Government will agree to amendments to make the Bill more palatable to its opponents) or it will set forth to the crossbench and try to convince enough of them to vote for the Bill that it can pass despite the Opposition's resistance.

Here's the maths: there are 76 Senators. In order to get a Bill through, the mover of the Bill needs to win a majority of Senators to support it. If the mover gets fewer than half the votes, or if there's a tied vote, the Bill is deemed to have failed.

During the 47th Parliament, the Senate was a gloriously colourful bouquet of diverse characters. There were 25 Government (Labor) Senators, and 30 Opposition (Liberal/ National Coalition) ones. Then there were 11 Greens Senators, two on Pauline Hanson's team, one Jacqui Lambie Network Senator (conveniently named Jacqui Lambie), one United Australia Party Senator (that's the Clive Palmer party) and then a further six Independents.

So that's a crossbench of 21. Nearly as many Senators as the Government has!

You can imagine how complex the negotiations were when the Government was trying to wheedle enough crossbenchers over the line to get its Bills through. The 2025 election made things a bit more straightforward for the Labor Government. Labor won some extra Senate spots, meaning it could get Bills through the Senate with the support of the Greens alone, and without having to go knocking on the doors of all the different Independents. Which means the game of 'Bunnies in a Basket' got a bit simpler in the 48th Parliament.

Bunnies in a Basket

Here's how it might work if the Government of the 47th Parliament was trying to get the Eliminating Maternal Embarrassment Bill 2025 through the Senate, and the Opposition was refusing to support it.

Imagine the Bill is a basket and the Senators are ***bunnies***.

There are 76 Senators and, if they all show up to vote, the Government needs 39 votes to clinch the deal. It has 25 of its own votes already. So that means it needs 14 more to get to the magic number. Through negotiation and strategy, the Government needs to persuade 14 more bunnies to hop into the legislative basket.

First port of call might be the Greens, because they have the biggest chunk of votes – if the Government can get the Greens to agree, that's 11 more bunnies in the basket. Only another three to collect!

But the Government might have to make concessions to win the Greens' support. The negotiations are often carried out by the Government's leader in the Senate, in conjunction with the minister involved, and sometimes – when things get very hairy – the Prime Minister. Let's imagine the discussion when the Government's Senate leader goes to visit the Greens:

Senate leader: *Could you please support our Bill to ban Annabel Crabb from using teen slang?*

Greens: *Hmmm. We're open to the idea of banning Annabel Crabb from using the word 'slay' and so on, because we are the party with the highest levels of support from young people because young people tend to be horrified at the extreme mess that older generations have made of the planet. So, we instinctively disapprove of older people adding insult to injury by stealing cool words from the youth and making them utterly cringe.*

Senate leader: *SLAY! Ahem, I mean, marvellous. Thank you. I'll count on your 11 votes then.*

Greens: *Not so fast, friend. Now that you're proposing new rules to apply at the national broadcaster, there's actually a couple of other things young people would like to see. A ban on* Midsomer Murders *repeats, for example. Also, we want a clause directing the ABC to do ten hours of programming every week specifically about the effects of climate change. If you support those amendments, we'll vote for the Bill.*

Senate leader (sweating lightly): *Ahhh, let me get back to you.*

Please remember, I'm just using a silly example to illustrate how the process works because if I used a real example, like the Finance Sector Reform Bill or something, you might actually lose consciousness. Also, I have a cartoonist to keep happy, which is why I keep mentioning bunnies.

Now the Government has 11 extra bunnies in the basket, but ***only*** if their conditions are met.

The Senate leader still has to go hunting for three more bunnies. They go to Pauline Hanson, who says, 'Actually, I'm a free speech purist and I'm opposed to the

Bill for that reason. But if you add a clause to defund the ABC completely, I'll think about it.'

Oof, too hard. If that particular bunny jumps in the basket, all the other bunnies will jump out!

Then maybe the Senate leader goes knocking on the doors of the other minor parties and Independents.

United Australia Party Senator: *Well, I'm okay with banning Annabel Crabb from saying stuff, but I'll be hopping mad if I have to support more publicly subsidised whining about climate change. How about some Donald Trump documentaries?*

Can't add this bunny to the basket.

Jacqui Lambie: *Don't you touch a hair on* Midsomer Murders' *head. That's my favourite show and heaps of Tasmanians watch it, so if you come for that show, I'll rip you a new one, champ. End of story.*

Can't add this bunny either.

This is the exciting thing about Bunnies in a Basket. Sometimes, the things you have to do to get new bunnies in the basket will cause other bunnies to hop out again! This is why being the Government leader in the Senate is such a hard job. The Consideration in Detail step of the Senate debate – where the Senators go through every clause and add amendments – can get very busy under these circumstances.

The Office of Parliamentary Counsel is usually standing by to help the crossbenchers draft their amendments. Pieces of paper fly around the Senate, and the Clerk keeps track of every single one of them. Each amendment has to be voted in or out, and it can get very hard to follow, especially if you're a new Senator. Or, of course, if you're just **very, very tired**.

Negotiations sometimes come right down to the wire. For a particularly tricky or controversial Bill the Senate may sit late into the night, especially if it's the last sitting session before a parliamentary break and the Government is determined to get its Bill through.

The longest single session in the Senate's history was when the Senate sat without a break for **28 hours and 56 minutes**, debating the Commonwealth Electoral Amendment Bill 2016 in March of that year. South Australian Independent Senator Nick Xenophon wore pyjamas into the chamber and took a pillow in too, to protest the Government's fiendish determination to push the Bill through at all costs.

Sometimes, in its desperation, the Government will make a deal with crossbench Senators to give them something else entirely unrelated in return for their support on a Bill under consideration. This is like if your parents offered you an hour of screen time in return for you eating your broccoli. Totally unrelated undertakings, but a powerful deal nonetheless because everybody walks away with something that makes them happy. This is basically what political dealmaking is about.

Deal or No Deal: Some Immortal Moments in Senate Negotiations

1996 Senator Brian Harradine agrees to approve the sale of one-third of Telstra in return for $350 million for environmental and telecommunications projects in his home state of Tasmania.

2009 After a tense stand-off, South Australian Independent Senator Nick Xenophon supplies the Rudd Government with the last vote it needs to secure $42 billion in government spending during the Global Financial Crisis. Senator Xenophon's price? Just $900 million in spending on the Murray–Darling River system in his home state.

2016 Liberal Democrat Senator David Leyonhjelm claims to have made a deal with the Coalition Abbott Government to pass its Bill creating a Building and Construction Commission in exchange for lifting restrictions on the importation of the Adler lever-action rifle.

Voting

Voting in Parliament – especially on legislation – is one of the most important and powerful things the House of Representatives or the Senate can do. So, there's a very formal process that's observed. It's not just a quick show of hands. It's intense – especially when the numbers are tight.

Voting happens in two ways. The first way is 'on the voices' where the Speaker (in the House of Representatives) or the President (in the Senate) will call out the motion being voted on and say, 'All those in favour say, "Aye!"'

And everyone who's voting yes will kind of mumble, 'Aye.'

The Speaker or President will then say, 'All those opposed say, "No!"'

At this point you'll either hear more mumbling or a chorus of voices shouting, 'NO!!'

The Speaker or President (the Chair) will then call the result by saying, for example, 'I think the Ayes have it!' And if everyone accepts that, the vote will be recorded, and the chamber moves on to the next thing.

Most parliamentary votes are done this way. It's quick, and it's reliable because on most issues, everyone including the Speaker or President knows where everyone stands.

If you're in the House of Representatives, for example, the vote will probably go whichever way the Government wants, because the Government has more MPs.

If a vote is carried on the voices, there's no record of who voted for what; just a note that the motion was passed or rejected.

But sometimes, MPs will yell, 'The Noes have it!!!' in response to the decision of the Chair. They might do this even though they know the Ayes have won, and that's usually because they want the exact record of who voted for and against the motion recorded in Hansard.

So, when the Speaker or President's call is challenged loudly by MPs, they will then ask, 'Is a division required?' and at that point people tend to bellow, 'Yes!' That is the cue for the more formal type of parliamentary voting called a **division**.* The call has to be challenged by more than one MP for a division to be triggered, but two is enough. Sometimes, when Opposition MPs are feeling especially miffed, they might call on divisions just to annoy the Government and jam up the day. It really works – divisions take a ***long*** time, so the degree of annoyance is quite high. Also, minor parties and Independents sometimes call for divisions when they are opposed to something that the two major parties – the Government and the Opposition – are banding together to support.

When divisions occur, Hansard records the name of every MP and whether they voted Aye or No. And when only a handful of MPs vote against a Bill that otherwise has overwhelming support, those MPs sometimes like to have their brave, doomed stance recorded for posterity.

These stances sometimes make their way into future election campaign pamphlets advertising that 'I, alone, stood up for the endangered Swift Parrot', or whatever it was they stood up for, however fruitlessly.

Divisions

Once a division has been called for, the Speaker or President heaves a brief sigh of resignation (at least, I imagine they do) and issues the command to 'Ring the bells!', whereupon the Clerk leans down and presses a button, and the bells of the Parliament begin their nagging, incessant ringing. The MPs and Senators have four minutes to return to the chamber, at which time the doors are locked.

The division bells ringing is a difficult thing to miss. As well as the sound, every single clock in Parliament House – and remember, there are more than 2700 of them – has two little flashing lights installed on its face. One is green, and one is red. When the Senate bells are rung, the clocks flash red and every Senator in the building knows they have to drop everything and run. When the flashing light's green, it's the Reps who have to bolt. Sometimes, when Parliament is super busy (more often towards the end of a sitting period, where they're smashing through Bills at top speed) you can get two sets of bells ringing at once, and every clock in the joint is flashing red and green and you'll see MPs and Senators hurling themselves down stairwells and puffing along corridors. These moments are not relaxing for anyone. In fact, in longer-serving politicians, the impulse to start running as soon as a bell starts ringing is so ingrained that even a random doorbell chime makes them jumpier than a greyhound at a pistol club.

The four-minute limit is enforced very strictly. If MPs get there too late, they don't get to vote, and if it happens to be a close vote and their non-appearance causes their party to lose a vote they should have won...well, **there is no greater disgrace**. Parliamentary parties have a special person called the Whip, an MP who is chosen and appointed to the person of making sure every MP knows when a vote is coming up and where they're supposed to be. It's the Whip who lets MPs know when they're allowed to go home. And it's the Whip who gets incredibly cross when they mess up.

One of the most famous tales concerning MPs missing divisions and attracting the scorn of their Whips and colleagues involves former Prime Minister Tony Abbott, who early in 2009 – during the Rudd Labor Government – was feeling a little blue about being cast into Opposition after his active years as a minister in the Howard Coalition Government. Mr Abbott retired to the parliamentary dining room with some colleagues and consumed a few consolatory glasses of wine, then reclined on the sofa in his office and conked out, missing a series of votes on the spending of several billion dollars. '*I lay down and next thing I knew it was morning,*' he recalled later. Mr Abbott was not popular with his Whip, or indeed with his party leader, Malcolm Turnbull. But later that year he successfully challenged Mr Turnbull for the leadership of the Liberal Party, and he went on to win an election and become Australia's 28th Prime Minister, so it would be wrong to say that his career was terribly affected in the long term.

FUN FACT: at the beginning of a new Parliament, when offices are being assigned, the Whips quietly make sure that the offices furthest from the chamber are occupied by their fittest MPs. If you're a little older or slower, your chances of a nice close office are greatly enhanced.

Doors Locked! What Now?

Back to the business of voting. Once the doors are locked, the Speaker or President directs MPs voting 'yes' to the motion at hand to 'pass to the right of the Chair' and those voting 'no' to pass to the left.

There is no way, in other words, of hiding how you vote. MPs voting yes sit on one side of the chamber and those voting no sit on the other side. 'Tellers' are appointed to count and double count how many yeses and noes there are, and everyone's name is noted. The result is then read out. If there is a series of votes in quick succession and everyone is already in the chamber, the Speaker or President can decide to just ring the bells for one minute for the second and successive votes, rather than for the full four minutes. This policy is quite a relief in busy weeks.

One Weird Thing You Might See During a Division

If an MP wants to talk to the Speaker while a division is underway, it is customary for that MP to hold a piece of paper over their head while they talk. It's obviously not normal human behaviour to hold a bit of paper over your head, unless you are very sunburn-prone and you find yourself unexpectedly at the tennis without a hat, so why do they do it?

The answer is that it's a custom derived from a British parliamentary tradition. In the British House of Commons, the way to attract the Speaker's attention is to stand up. During a division, however, lots of MPs are on their feet so it's hard for the Speaker to tell who is wanting to speak, and who's just ambling over to the right or left side of the Chair for the division. In the old days, when the House of Commons was filled almost exclusively with well-to-do chaps, they all wore top hats. So in order to distinguish himself from other standing MPs during a division, a chap wanting a word with the Speaker would simply clap on his top hat and state his business. As top hats fell out of favour, MPs took to covering their heads with whatever came to hand – most usually, ***a piece of paper***. And somehow, this faintly ridiculous tradition survived all the way through to present-day Canberra.

While a division is underway, MPs stroll all over the place, out of their usual seats – Government MPs sit on the Opposition benches and vice versa. This is why it's very unwise to keep a messy desk in the chamber. If you're a minister, you really don't want an Opposition MP to come across the notes for your cunning plan while they're briefly perching in your spot during a division.

If All Else Fails – Form a Committee!

Sometimes, MPs and Senators may decide they need more information on a Bill. Or they might feel they want to hear the specific views of community groups, or industry groups, or ordinary people who might be affected by the proposed laws. Or perhaps they might be looking for a way to delay things a little bit! So, they vote to send the Bill off to be examined by a parliamentary committee.

Both the House of Representatives and the Senate have special committees of MPs that are devoted to particular subject areas – defence and foreign affairs, for instance, or communications, or community services. They travel around and take evidence from expert witnesses and when directed by the Parliament, they can hold a special inquiry into a particular Bill to investigate what its possible effects might be, beyond what the minister has said they will be. Committees will comprise MPs and/or Senators from a variety of party backgrounds. They are actually a good opportunity for politicians of opposing views to work together and get to know each other better, which is quite a useful thing.

Once the committee has completed its inquiry into a Bill, a report is submitted, everyone reads it, then the legislative process gets back underway.

And they provide an excellent way for voters, organisations and business groups to inform the Parliament what's going on around Australia.

STEP SEVEN: BACK TO THE LOWER HOUSE

Nearly there!

Once the amendments have been debated and voted on in the Senate, and each clause has been accepted and rejected, the final version of the Bill is approved and sent back to the Lower House. If the Bill hasn't been amended at all, this part is straightforward – the House already agreed with it, so the Bill has satisfied the requirement that it pass both houses of Parliament in the same form. Hurrah! It gets checked and certified by the Clerk, then it's off to the Governor-General in Yarralumla, Canberra (the official residence of the Governor-General) for Royal assent.

However, if the Senate has amended the Bill during the negotiation process with the crossbench, for example, the House of Representatives has to approve the exact amendments if the Bill is to become law.

The Government has two choices. It can cop the changes, swallow its pride and decide that the amended version is better than no version – in which case, the House will vote to approve the amended form of the Bill. This means both Houses agree to identical versions of the Bill, which is then checked and certified, and hustled out to Yarralumla as above.

Or the Government can pick a fight with the Senate by stripping out the amendments, returning the Bill to its previous form, and sending it back to the Senate asking it to reconsider. If the Senate then votes to insist on its amendments, they have quite a situation. The Bill cannot become law, because the two Houses are in disagreement about exactly what it should say.

The Bill doesn't just keep pinging back and forth between Houses indefinitely, keeping the Serjeant-at-Arms's step count up. The Government has to wait; after a period of three months, it can try again. And if the Senate continues to insist on its alterations, it's what's known as ***legislative deadlock***.

In these circumstances, the Government may put the whole thing into the too-hard basket and set the Bill aside.

But if enough of these contested Bills pile up, the Government has the option of an extreme course of action. It can call a ***'double dissolution election'***, in which every Senate and House of Representatives seat is declared vacant, an election is held, new representatives elected, and the Bills reconsidered in a special joint sitting of the new Parliament in which all the MPs and Senators cram into the one chamber and vote all together.

While Australia has had many double dissolution elections, the joint sitting of Parliament has only happened once in Australian history. In August 1974, after multiple pieces of legislation proposed by the Whitlam Government were rejected by the conservative-dominated Senate, a double dissolution election took place. The joint sitting dealt with six contested Bills on subjects ranging from electoral reform to health insurance. The Whitlam Government was re-elected, and the laws were passed by the joint sitting. But the Whitlam Government didn't last much more than a year after that – it was dismissed by Governor-General Sir John Kerr in November 1975, in what is known as the Dismissal, and remains the single most controversial political upheaval in the history of the Federation.

Some Frequently Asked Questions

Passing a Bill seems kind of exhausting. How often does it happen?

According to our excellent friends at the Parliamentary Education Office, the average number of Bills introduced and passed each year is 140.

But honestly? There have been a lot of fluctuations in the annual Bill-count over the years since Federation. Some Governments are a hive of activity and produce a lot of legislation. Others are a bit more chilled out.

The highest number of Bills passed by the Parliament in a calendar year was in 1992, when Paul Keating was Prime Minister and burst into a ***legislative frenzy***, having displaced his colleague Bob Hawke from the top job. In that year, the Parliament passed 262 new laws.

The snooziest year for legislation, by contrast, was 1907. Alfred Deakin was having his second crack at being Prime Minister that year, and the Parliament passed only 12 new laws. In his defence, Deakin spent a good chunk of 1907 sailing to London and back to attend an Imperial Conference to see about buying some naval destroyers. In those days, foreign visits chewed up a lot of prime ministerial time.

Can you speed up the process?

Yep, you can. To get more Bills processed more quickly, the Parliament will sometimes move the debate to the Federation Chamber. This means more than one Bill can be debated at the same time.

Towards the end of a parliamentary sitting period, the Bills can start to pile up, especially if they've required complex negotiations along the way. Negotiators often like to keep their cards close to their chests until late in the game. And combined with the universal human tendency to leave hard things to the very last minute – ***Bingo!*** You get a final parliamentary sitting week that's absolutely crammed with Bills all needing attention.

In these circumstances, to speed things along, the Government may impose what's called a 'guillotine'.

Now, while this does sound like an excitingly French Revolution–themed programme of activities, the reality is that a 'guillotine' is a motion that chops speaking times, not actual necks.

A 'guillotine' is where a minister moves a motion that the chamber declare 'That the Bill be considered an urgent Bill'. The minister then sets time limits for the remaining stages of debate. It means that not everyone will get to speak and that speaking times will be limited.

This decision rarely goes down well with Oppositions, who invariably protest that restricting debate is a grotesque violation of democratic principles. Which it definitely is.

But poking through the history books reveals that both the Labor Party and the Liberal Party when in government have engaged in this particular brand of democratic violation when it suited them. ***Viva la guillotine!***

The Standing Orders – the Parliament's large and detailed book of rules – outlines restrictions on speaking times for speeches on Bills, questions and answers. In the early days of the Australian Parliament, there were no time limits on speeches that MPs made, but on 13 November 1918, when the New South Wales Senator Albert Gardiner rose to speak on the Commonwealth Electoral Bill 1918, the seeds were sown for parliamentary time limits.

Gardiner – a former carpenter and passionate free-trader – spoke for 12 hours and 40 minutes on the Bill, whose major proposal was the introduction of preferential voting (see Chapter 4). He was annoyed that the Government was pushing the legislation through with unseemly haste, so while his fellow Senators snoozed or nipped out for a snack, Gardiner read out the entire Bill including all its schedules and attachments. It didn't make any difference; the Bill went through. But the following year, the Standing Orders were amended to prevent MPs from making limitless speeches.

A FINAL WORD FROM SHAWN

Hey team, that's it!

But it's not the whole story of Parliament House, or the democratic system that lives here. It's barely even the beginning.

The history of this continent, and the people who have lived here for millennia, organising themselves, living together, finding out ways to fix problems and invent things and try to make things fair is a long history.

Compared to that, the Commonwealth of Australia is still brand-new. And it's changed a lot even in the short time since it was created in 1901, and it will continue to change and evolve. Maybe you'll change it? Maybe you'll make it fairer, or better. Or maybe you won't change it. Maybe you'll just be a voter and a citizen. In a democracy like ours, these are both powerful things to be.

Like most Australians, I'm a blow-in. I'm only here because I was trapped in a chunk of limestone that became a floor in Parliament House in the 1980s. In terms of the history of Australia, I'm a rank newcomer. But as fossilised marine organisms go, I'm on the opinionated side. So, I'm going to leave you with my favourite things about Australia's system of government.

This is what it is to be human. Humans make mistakes – always have and always will. It's easy for me to say, as a crustacean. But the most important thing is to learn from mistakes. And to be open, always, to the views of others.

Democracies are imperfect. That's because they are made up of imperfect people, otherwise known as just 'people'. And in a democracy, you have to listen to other people. Everyone gets a vote. Sometimes you win, sometimes you lose, but you keep showing up.

Shawn's Top Five Favourite Things About Australia's Democracy

1) Secret Ballot

Australians invented the secret ballot – the idea of filling out a ballot paper without anyone standing over your shoulder yelling at you or bullying you to vote one way or another. This is important, because it means to win your vote, a candidate has to win your trust and faith, not just make you scared. This is a core part of democracy. And it started here!

2) Compulsory Voting

Not many countries in the world have it, but when you make voting compulsory, you're insisting that all citizens are full citizens. You're not just asking people to pay tax and obey laws, you're asking them to take part even if they're shy, or poor, or don't speak English perfectly. And when poor people and sick people and young people and old people and immigrants all have to vote, you're also making sure that politicians take those people and their concerns seriously, because their votes count just as much as everybody else's.

3) Preferential Voting

Not everyone's a fan and it's complicated to explain, but no other country uses preferential voting as enthusiastically as we do. It gives Australian voters an opportunity to express a detailed opinion about the people who are asking for our votes.

4) The Australian Electoral Commission

We tend to take the Australian Electoral Commission for granted. But Australia was the ***first country in the world*** to install a permanent, independent authority to run all our elections. And having a neutral organisation in charge of elections is a really important part of maintaining trust in the system!

5) Fairness

As a democracy we haven't always been perfect at being fair, but Australians were great at recognising early on that it wasn't fair to only give rich people the vote. And great at spotting that it wasn't fair to only give men the vote. It took longer to work out that blocking people from voting – or from coming to Australia – just because of their race was terribly unfair. But there will always be rules or laws from our past that we look back at now and feel bad or embarrassed about, among all the stuff there is to be proud of.

GLOSSARY

Act of Parliament: A Bill that has been made law by being passed by both Houses of the Australian Parliament.

Backbencher: The Members of Parliament or Senators who sit in the back of the House or Senate.

Bicameral parliament: A parliament with two Houses. In Australia, these are the House of Representatives and the Senate.

Bill: A draft Act of Parliament that is in the process of being discussed and voted on in Parliament.

Black Rod: A staff made of ebony wood with a silver crown on top that symbolises the power of the Usher of the Black Rod.

Cabinet: The group of about 21 high-level politicians including the Prime Minister who have specific responsibilities in governing Australia.

Candidate: A person who runs for political office.

Caucus: A meeting of the Labor Party MPs.

Clerk of the House: The most senior parliamentary official in the House of Representatives who advises the Speaker and Members of Parliament.

Coalition: An agreement between two or more parties to create a bigger group and strengthen their position in Parliament. In Australian politics the term means the partnership between the Liberal Party of Australia, the Liberal National Party of Queensland and the National Party.

Commonwealth: The national parliament and government of Australia, representing all the states and territories together.

Convicts: In Australia this means the prisoners who were transported to Australia from Britain and Ireland from 1788 and up until 1868.

Defamation: The act of publishing false information that ruins someone's reputation.

Deficit: An economic term when the government spends more than it earns.

Dictator: A type of ruler who makes all the decisions about running a country without consulting anyone else.

Divisions: Formal recorded votes by the Members of Parliament in Parliament.

Double Dissolution: When both Houses (the House of Representatives and the Senate) are shut down by the Governor-General, usually on the advice of the Prime Minister because they cannot get bills through the Parliament, to force an election.

Formal Vote: A correctly filled out ballot paper that is counted during an election.

Frontbencher: Generally the ministers and shadow ministers who sit on the front bench of the House or the Senate.

Gin Acts of the 1700s: The British government's response to the so-called 'Gin Craze' in Britain where it passed a series of laws to control how much gin was being drunk.

Governor-General: Australia's Head of State and the King (or Queen) of the United Kingdom's representative in Australia's Parliament.

Hansard: The official written account of everything that is said in Parliament.

High Court: The uppermost law court in Australia where issues of national significance are decided related to interpreting the Australian Constitution.

House of Representatives: Also known as the Lower House, the House of Representatives is one of two Houses in Australia's Parliament and has 150 members including the Prime Minister.

Hung Parliament: When there are small numbers of politicians from both major political parties in the House of Representatives and no party has the majority.

Inflation: An economic term to describe the price of goods going up.

Informal Vote: An incorrectly filled out ballot paper that cannot be counted towards the election result.

KGB: The name of the secret police and intelligence agency in the Soviet Union (USSR) from the 1950s to the early 1990s.

Mace: An ornate solid silver staff with a thick end and gold plating that symbolises royal authority, the authority of the House of Representatives and the Speaker of the House.

Minister: A member of the government who has an area of responsibility.

Opposition: The political party that did not get enough seats in the House of Representatives to form a government but that has the next most seats in the House.

Party Room: The actual room in Parliament House where a party's MPs meet, and sometimes just a description of the party's MPs meeting together.

Penal Colony: Settlements established by colonial powers such as Britain, in places such as Australia, to imprison and punish convicts.

Portfolio: Also called a department, this is the name given to a minister's area of responsibility.

Premier: The elected leader of an Australian state. (The elected leader of an Australian territory is called the Chief Minister.)

President of the Senate: The Senator, elected by their colleagues in the Senate, who chairs meetings and makes sure that the Senators follow the rules, also known as Standing Orders.

Press Gallery: Both the name of the group of journalists who report on Parliament and the place where they work in Parliament House.

Prime Minister: The leader of the Australian Government.

Question Time: A daily allotted time for politicians to ask questions of ministers, which they must answer.

Rail gauges: The space between railway tracks on which the train's wheels sit.

Referendum: A vote by the people on a proposed change to the Australian Constitution.

Senate: Also known as the Upper House, the Senate is one of two Houses in Parliament and has 76 members.

Senator: A person elected to the Senate.

Serjeant-at-Arms: The officer who assists in the running of the House of Representatives. Carries the mace at the beginning and end of each sitting day.

Shadow Minister: A member of the Opposition assigned to a department to closely watch the work of the corresponding minister in the Government.

Speaker of the House: The presiding officer in the House of Representatives who chairs meetings and makes sure that everyone follows the rules. They are elected by their colleagues in the House and expected to treat everyone equally.

Stamp Duty: A tax levied by a government for certain financial transactions like selling a house.

Surplus: An economic term meaning the leftover money after the budget (money) has been spent.

The Dismissal: An event in 1975 when the Whitlam Government was sacked by the Governor-General Sir John Kerr, which caused a constitutional crisis.

Treason: The act of betraying a country, like trying to overthrow a government or a monarch.

Unicameral parliament: A government with only one House in which all the laws and rules are made.

Usher of the Black Rod: The officer who works in the Senate whose responsibilities include carrying the Black Rod and escorting the President of the Senate into and out of the Senate.

Westminster-style democracy: A method of parliamentary government based on the structure of Britain's government.

WHAT TO SPOT IN PARLIAMENT HOUSE

Beehives: Three beehives can be found in the native landscape around Parliament House. Parliament House even has its own beekeeper!

Blue carpet: Oops! You need to get out of here! This is the Executive Wing.

Ducks: Look where you put your feet! They like to poop.

Fountains: With a friend, find a seat next to a fountain in one of the courtyards. Ask another friend to eavesdrop on you both chatting, then ask them what you said. I bet they'll struggle!

Glass security huts: These are from the 1980s with phones that are actually joined to the wall with cords.

Green carpet: You are in the House of Representatives.

Magna Carta: One of only three copies of Magna Carta known to be outside Britain. Purchased by the Australian Government in 1952, it dates back to 1297.

Magpies: Watch your head during spring! They like to swoop.

Mosaic: The 196-square-metre mosaic *Possum and Wallaby Dreaming* by Warlpiri artist Kumantje (Michael Nelson) Jagamara AM is in the Forecourt.

Moths: If you are lucky, you might see a migrating bogong moth – but keep your mouth closed.

Native Australian flowers made of intricate filigreed timbers: There are 20 marquetry panels depicting Australian flora in the Marble Foyer.

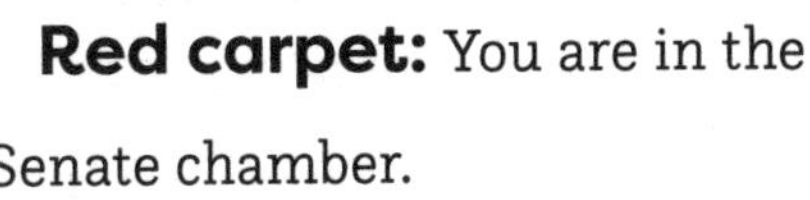

Red carpet: You are in the Senate chamber.

Shawn the Prawn: This fossil is clearly visible at the base of the stairs of the Marble Foyer.

The Australian Coat of Arms: There are numerous depictions of our Coat of Arms in Parliament House. One is above the main entrance. How many more can you spot?

The Big Picture: Otherwise known as *The Opening of the First Parliament of the Commonwealth of Australia by His Royal Highness the Duke of Cornwall and York, 9 May 1901*. This painting by artist Tom Roberts depicts the first ever sitting of Parliament. You can't miss it in the Main Committee Room.

The Great Hall Tapestry: One of the largest tapestries in the world and a collaboration between artist Arthur Boyd, architectural firm Mitchell/Giurgla & Thorp, and the craftspeople of the Victorian Tapestry Workshop. Can you spot the cockatoo?

TIMELINE OF AUSTRALIAN PRIME MINISTERS

Australia has had 31 prime ministers since Federation in 1901.

1901–1903 .... Edmund Barton

1903–1910 (three times) .... Alfred Deakin

1904 .... Chris Watson

1904–1905 .... George Reid

1908–1915 (three times) .... Andrew Fisher

1913–1914 .... Joseph Cook

1915–1923 (three times) .... Billy Hughes

1923–1929 .... Stanley Bruce

1929–1932 .... James Scullin

1932–1939 .... Joseph Lyons

1939	Earle Page
1939–1966 **(two times)**	Robert Menzies
1941	Arthur Fadden
1941–1945	John Curtin
1945	Frank Forde
1945–1949	Ben Chifley
1966–1967	Harold Holt
1967–1968	John McEwen
1968–1971	John Gorton
1971–1972	Billy McMahon
1972–1975	Gough Whitlam
1975–1983	Malcom Fraser
1983–1991	Bob Hawke
1991–1996	Paul Keating
1996–2007	John Howard
2007–2013 **(two times)**	Kevin Rudd
2010–2013	Julia Gillard
2013–2015	Tony Abbott
2015–2018	Malcolm Turnbull
2018–2022	Scott Morrison
2022–	Anthony Albanese

SOURCES

Chapter 1

p24: https://www.parliament.vic.gov.au/about/history-and-heritage/our-living-heritage/the-story-behind-the-story/

Chapter 2

p39: Brett, J. (2019). *From Secret Ballot to Democracy Sausage: How Australia Got Compulsory Voting*. Melbourne: Text Publishing.

p43: https://peo.gov.au/understand-our-parliament/history-of-parliament/federation/the-federation-of-australia

p49: 'INCIDENT OF THE DAY.', *The Age* (Melbourne, Vic.: 1854 –1954), 2 January 1901, p. 7.
Access via http://nla.gov.au/nla.news-article196062033

Chapter 3

p53: https://www.aph.gov.au/constitution

p77: https://www.aph.gov.au/constitution

p78: https://www.smh.com.au/politics/federal/constitutional-crisis-leaves-turnbull-government-fighting-for-its-political-life-20170818-gxzi5c.html

Chapter 5

pp123-124: https://budget.gov.au/

p127: https://www.smh.com.au/entertainment/tv-and-radio/laurie-oakes-veteran-political-journalist-retires-aged-73-20170803-gxojye.html

Chapter 6

p134: https://pressgallery.net.au/history-2/

p140: https://pressgallery.net.au/history-2/

p141: https://www.aph.gov.au/-/media/05_About_Parliament/54_Parliamentary_Depts/544_Parliamentary_Library/firsteight/deakin/Alfred-Deakins-letters-London-Morning-Post-Volume-3.pdf

p157: https://www.aph.gov.au/About_Parliament/Senate/Publications_and_resources/Papers_and_research/Papers_on_Parliament_and_other_resources/Papers_on_Parliament/64/c01

p158: Park, S., Fisher, C., McGuinness, K., Lee, J., McCallum, K., Cai, X., Chatskin, M., Mardjianto, L. & Yao, P. (2024). *Digital News Report: Australia 2024*. Canberra: News and Media Research Centre, University of Canberra. DOI: https://doi.org/10.60836/fxcr-xq72

Chapter 7

p165: https://www.theguardian.com/australia-news/2018/sep/19/australian-pm-threatens-strawberry-saboteurs-with-15-years-in-jail

p193: *The House with Annabel Crabb*, Season 1, Episode 5, ABC iView

p199: https://peo.gov.au/

FURTHER READING

This book is really just a tiny taste of our Federation and its workings. If you are hungry for more, whether it's Australian history or information on the Parliament, one of the best things you can do is go to a library and ask your friendly local librarian for further reading ideas!

If you go to ABC iView, you can watch the series *The House With Annabel Crabb*, which shows you the inside life of the Parliament. Or our new show, *Annabel Crabb's Civic Duty*, which looks at the history of our democracy and visits some of the stories in this book.

From Secret Ballot to Democracy Sausage by Judith Brett (2019) is a wonderful book and will give you deeper detail about some of the unique features of our system.

The Parliamentary Education Office has all manner of fact sheets and research, which are very clear and helpful. **peo.gov.au**

AIATSIS has some great resources on the Indigenous Nations who have cared for and governed this continent for a lot longer than the Parliament's been around. **aiatsis.gov.au**

I drew some of the stories about the old Press Gallery from Nick Haggerty's excellent essay on the Federal Parliamentary Press Gallery's website. Worth a read! **pressgallery.net.au/history-2**

And if you're interested in podcasts, I'd heartily recommend *Hey History* – it's an Australian history podcast made by kids for kids. Check it out!

ACKNOWLEDGEMENTS

Thank you to Allen & Unwin's Anna McFarlane, who noticed way back in 2017 that there was a gap for a readable book for children about how the Parliament works, and asked if I'd think about writing one. Eight years and a pandemic later – here it is! Sorry about the wait, Anna. Thank you for your patience with the delay, and thank you to senior editor Nicola Santilli, designer Kristy Lund-White and the whole team at Allen & Unwin.

Of course, 'thank you' seems a paltry phrase to encompass the vast and blush-inducing honour of sharing a printed page with First Dog on the Moon, a cartoonist of gentle and savage genius. But let's go with it.

Thank you to former senator Amanda Vanstone, whose SA essay competition for high schoolers in the 1980s gave me my first introduction to Parliament House and sparked a fascination I haven't quite kicked yet.

Thank you to the humans of Parliament, the Press Gallery colleagues, the redoubtable Parliamentary Education Office on whose resources I so regularly draw, and to the wonderful Museum of Australian Democracy, whose Acting Head of Museum Experience and Learning, Dr Stephanie Smith, kindly assisted with an expert read of the manuscript.

Thank you to the immortal Judith Brett (whose book *From Secret Ballot to Democracy Sausage* is in my forever top ten). And thank you to my ABC colleagues who've infested Parliament with me over the years, most particularly Madeleine Hawcroft who helped to conceive and research this book, and who with the brilliant director Stamatia Maroupas has been my long-term collaborator on matters political, from *Kitchen Cabinet* to documentaries like *The House, Ms Represented* and our latest and newest, *Annabel Crabb's Civic Duty*, the idea for which came to me while working on this book. On *The House* and *Civic Duty* I was much aided – and always entertained – by the curious minds of researchers Farz Edraki, Carolyn Cage, Julia O'Shea and Georgia Roberts, and as always by the wonderful ABC librarian Cathy Beale – an institutional treasure.

Thank you to my agent Fiona Inglis, to my partner Jeremy, and to my own three children, who not only did not get this book in time for their own Year 6 excursions to Parliament, but also had to put up with me disappearing to my desk to finish the thing. I love you.

ANNABEL CRABB

Annabel Crabb is an ABC writer and presenter who has covered Australian politics for nearly 25 years as a news reporter and columnist. She is the creator and presenter of *Ms Represented*, presenter and writer for the ABC-wide *Australia Talks* project, and co-host of the initial and 2021 return series of *Tomorrow Tonight*, with Charlie Pickering. She has written and presented the documentary series on life inside parliament, *The House with Annabel Crabb*. She created the political interview series *Kitchen Cabinet*, which she has presented for seven seasons on ABC TV, and for which she received two Logie nominations in 2013 including the Graham Kennedy Award for Most Outstanding New Talent and Most Popular New Female Talent.

Annabel is also host of the ABC Australian history and food series, *Back in Time for Dinner, Further Back in Time for Dinner* and *Back in Time for the Corner Shop*. She is a regular face on ABC TV's election night and Budget broadcasts and has a long history of appearances on ABC's *Insiders* program, including a stint as acting host in 2019.

She has won a Walkley Award for feature writing, with her Quarterly Essay entitled *Stop at Nothing: The Life and Adventures of Malcolm Turnbull*. She is a regular commentator across the ABC's radio network. With friend and ABC colleague Leigh Sales, Annabel hosts the podcast *Chat 10 Looks 3*, an independent podcast in which the pair discuss books, film, culture and cooking.

FIRST DOG ON THE MOON

First Dog on the Moon is Australia's only Walkley award-winning marsupial-based cartoonist and has done all sorts of things including books, radio, stage shows and a lot of lying down.

First Dog has been observing Australian politicians since primary school and was once the Museum of Australian Democracy's Cartoonist of the Year.

First Dog's documentation of politicians' exploits and adventures can be found in newspapers such as *Guardian Australia* and on **firstdogonthemoon.com.au**

INDEX

I ♡ DEMOCRACY